ANTI-INFLAMMATORY COOKBOOK FOR BEGINNERS:

Tasty and Delicious Recipes for a Healthier You.
Heal the Immune System, Reduce Inflammation, and Enjoy the Cooking

Samuel Witte

TABLE OF CONTENTS

WHAT IS AN
ANTI-INFLAMMATORY DIET?

Anti-Inflammatory eating is a diet that focuses on consuming foods that help reduce inflammation. Although inflammation is a normal response to injury or illness, it can lead to various health problems, such as autoimmune disorders, arthritis, and heart disease, when it persists over an extended period. An anti-inflammatory diet aims to provide the body with the nutrients it needs to reduce chronic inflammation and promote overall health and wellness. The body's natural response to illness or injury is to initiate inflammation. Still, if this response continues for an extended period, it can result in various health issues like arthritis, autoimmune disorders, and heart disease. It also restricts or limits the intake of processed and refined foods, added sugars, and unhealthy fats, contributing to inflammation in the body.

An anti-inflammatory diet aims to provide the body with the nutrients it needs to reduce inflammation and promote overall health and wellness. This approach emphasizes consuming whole, natural foods that are minimally processed, such as vegetables, fruits, lean proteins, whole grains, and healthy fats. It also reduces the intake of foods known to trigger inflammation, such as processed foods, sugar, and saturated and trans fats.

An anti-inflammatory diet can improve their overall health, boost their immune system, and reduce their risk of chronic diseases. In this cookbook, we will explore the principles of anti-inflammatory eating and provide recipes and meal plans to help you incorporate these principles into your daily diet.

What to eat?

 The Anti-Inflammatory Diet is focused on consuming whole, nutrient-dense foods that are believed to have anti-inflammatory properties. Some essential foods to incorporate into this diet include:

1. Fruits and Vegetables: Eating various colorful fruits and vegetables is essential for getting a wide range of vitamins, minerals, and antioxidants that help reduce inflammation.

2. Whole Grains: Whole grains, such as quinoa, brown rice, and whole wheat, are good sources of fiber, vitamins, and minerals, and they can help reduce inflammation.

3. Lean Protein: Foods like fish, chicken, and legumes are rich in anti-inflammatory omega-3 fatty acids, and they can help reduce inflammation in the body.

4. Healthy Fats: Foods like nuts, seeds, avocado, and olive oil are high in healthy monounsaturated and polyunsaturated fats that help reduce inflammation.

5. Spices: Certain spices, such as turmeric, ginger, and rosemary, have anti-inflammatory properties and can help reduce inflammation.

Limiting or avoiding processed foods, sugar, and unhealthy fats is also recommended, as these can contribute to inflammation in the body. This diet can support your overall health and well-being and potentially reduce the risk of certain chronic diseases.

What not to eat?

On an Anti-inflammatory diet, avoiding certain foods linked to inflammation in the body is recommended. These foods include:

1. Refined carbohydrates and sugar: Foods such as white bread, pasta, pastries, and sugary drinks can increase inflammation in the body.

2. Trans fats: In many processed foods, trans fats have been linked to increased inflammation and should be avoided.

3. Fried foods: Deep-fried foods, such as French fries, are high in trans fats and can increase inflammation.

4. Processed meats: Processed meats, such as sausages, ham, and bacon, contain preservatives and other chemicals that can increase inflammation.

5. Alcohol: Excessive alcohol consumption should be limited be can increase inflammation in the body and should be limited.

6. High-fat dairy products: Full-fat dairy products, such as cheese and whole milk, can increase inflammation in the body.

7. Refined vegetable oils: Refined vegetable oils, such as corn and soybean, are high in omega-6 fatty acids, which can increase inflammation in the body.

It's important to note that everyone's bodies react differently to certain foods, and it's essential to listen to your own body and adjust your diet accordingly.

Benefits of an Anti-inflammatory diet

The Anti-Inflammatory Diet is a way of eating designed to reduce inflammation levels. This diet focuses on consuming whole, nutrient-dense foods rich in anti-inflammatory nutrients and antioxidants while avoiding foods that trigger inflammation. Some of the key benefits of following an Anti-Inflammatory Diet include the following:

1. Improved joint health: Inflammation in the joints is a common cause of pain and discomfort, and an Anti-Inflammatory Diet can help reduce this inflammation and improve joint health.

2. Better heart health: Inflammation is also linked to heart-related issues, including heart disease and stroke. By reducing inflammation, the Anti-Inflammatory Diet may help improve heart health and reduce the risk of heart-related problems.

3. Better digestion: Inflammation in the gut is a common issue, and consuming an Anti-Inflammatory Diet can help reduce this inflammation and improve digestive health.

4. Better brain health: Inflammation in the brain has been linked to various neurological conditions, including depression, anxiety, and dementia. By reducing inflammation, the Anti-Inflammatory Diet may help improve the brain's health and reduce the risk of neurological problems.

5. Better skin health: Inflammation can also impact skin health, leading to acne and eczema. An Anti-Inflammatory Diet can help reduce inflammation and improve skin health.

6. Increased energy: By consuming a balanced diet rich in nutrients, following an Anti-Inflammatory Diet can help improve overall health and increase energy levels.

7. Weight management: The Anti-Inflammatory Diet promotes weight management and healthy weight loss by focusing on whole, nutrient-dense foods.

The Anti-Inflammatory Diet is a healthy eating method that can help reduce inflammation, improve health, and reduce the risk of chronic diseases.

Tips And Tricks for Making Anti-Inflammatory Eating A Part Of Your Daily Routine:

1. Start your day with a nourishing breakfast: A healthy breakfast sets the tone for the rest of the day, and starting with a meal rich in anti-inflammatory ingredients can help set you on the right path. Some options include oatmeal with berries and almond milk, a smoothie made with spinach, avocado, and almond butter, or a quinoa bowl with roasted vegetables and a poached egg.

2. Incorporate more plants into your meals: Plant-based foods are some of the most anti-inflammatory foods you can eat. Focus on eating a variety of colorful fruits and vegetables, as well as nuts, seeds, and whole grains.

3. Reduce your intake of processed foods: Foods can contain high amounts of sugar, unhealthy fats, and artificial additives that can contribute to inflammation in the body. Concentrate on consuming whole foods that are minimally processed rather than those that have undergone extensive processing.

4. Experiment with anti-inflammatory spices: Spices like turmeric, ginger, and garlic have powerful anti-inflammatory properties. Add them to your cooking to add flavor and boost the anti-inflammatory benefits of your meals.

5. You can be innovative by incorporating healthy fats into your diet, as they can reduce inflammation. Some sources of healthy fats include avocado, nuts, and olive oil. Incorporate more of these foods into your diet and use them as a source of healthy fat in your cooking.

6. Staying well-hydrated by drinking ample water throughout the day can aid in the removal of toxins from the body and alleviate inflammation. Aim for at least 7 cups of water daily, and consider adding herbal teas for added flavor and health benefits.

7. Plan: Planning your meals can help you stay on track with your anti-inflammatory eating plan. Make a grocery list, meal plan, and schedule time for food prep to help you stay organized and focused.

BREAKFAST

MEDITERRANEAN QUINOA SALAD

Preparation Time: 30 minutes
Cook time: 15
Servings: 4

Ingredients:

- 1 cup quinoa
- 2 cups water
- 1 can chickpeas, drained and rinsed
- 1 cup cherry tomatoes, halved
- 1 cup cucumber, diced
- 1/2 cup red onion, diced
- 1/4 cup kalamata olives, chopped
- 1/4 cup fresh parsley, chopped
- 1/4 cup fresh mint, chopped
- 3 tablespoons lemon juice
- 3 tablespoons extra virgin olive oil

- 1 teaspoon sea salt
- 1/2 teaspoon black pepper

Instructions:
1. Wash the quinoa and add it to a pot with 2 cups of water. Heat the contents until boiling, then reduce the heat and cover the pot. Allow the mixture to simmer for approximately 15-20 minutes or until the quinoa has softened and fully absorbed the water.
2. Combine the cooked quinoa with chickpeas, cherry tomatoes, cucumber, red onion, kalamata olives, parsley, and mint in a large mixing bowl.
3. Combine lemon juice, extra virgin olive oil, salt, and pepper in a small mixing bowl, then whisk the ingredients together.
4. Drizzle the dressing over the quinoa mixture, then stir until it is evenly coated.
5. Serve at room temperature or chill in the refrigerator for 30 minutes before serving.

Nutrition Information (per serving): Calories: 350 Fat: 17g Saturated Fat: 2.5g Carbohydrates: 41g Fiber: 8g Protein: 11g Sodium: 720mg

GRILLED SALMON WITH AVOCADO SALSA

Preparation Time: 15 minutes

Cook Time: 12 minutes

Servings: 4

Ingredients:

- 4 salmon fillets, about 6 ounces each
- 1 teaspoon paprika
- 1 teaspoon cumin
- 1 teaspoon garlic powder
- 1/2 teaspoon salt
- 1/4 teaspoon black pepper
- 1 avocado, diced
- 1/2 red onion, diced
- 1 jalapeno pepper, seeded and diced
- 2 tablespoons chopped fresh cilantro
- 2 tablespoons freshly squeezed lime juice
- 2 tablespoons olive oil

Instructions:
1. Mix the paprika, cumin, garlic powder, salt, and pepper in a small bowl.
2. Brush the salmon fillets with olive oil and sprinkle with the spice mixture.
3. Heat your grill or grill pan in advance to medium-high temperature.
4. Cook the salmon on the grill for 6-7 minutes on each side or until it appears opaque and can be easily separated using a fork.
5. While the salmon is cooking, mix the avocado, red onion, jalapeno, cilantro, lime juice, and olive oil in a medium bowl.
6. Serve the salmon topped with avocado salsa.

Nutrition Information (per serving): Calories: 385 Fat: 29g Protein: 26g Carbohydrates: 10g Fiber: 5g Sugar: 2g Sodium: 420mg Cholesterol: 62mg Saturated Fat: 4g

CINNAMON APPLE QUINOA PORRIDGE

Prep Time: 5 minutes

Cook Time: 15 minutes

Servings: 2

Ingredients:

- 1 cup quinoa
- 2 cups water
- 1 teaspoon cinnamon
- 1 medium apple, peeled and diced
- 2 tablespoons almonds, chopped
- 1 tablespoon honey
- 1 teaspoon vanilla extract

Instructions:

1. Wash the quinoa using a fine-mesh strainer and add it to a medium-sized saucepan with water.
2. Heat the mixture until it boils, then reduce the heat to a low setting and cover the saucepan with a lid.
3. Cook the quinoa for 15 minutes or until all the water has been absorbed.

4. Stir in the cinnamon, diced apple, chopped almonds, honey, and vanilla extract.
5. Serve hot, and enjoy!

Nutrition Information (per serving): Calories: 341 Fat: 8g Protein: 11g Carbohydrates: 60g Fiber: 7g

BREAKFAST BOWLS

Preparation Time: 10 minutes
Cook Time: 20 minutes
Servings: 4

Ingredients:

- 1 cup quinoa, rinsed
- 2 cups water
- 1 avocado, sliced
- 1 cup cherry tomatoes, halved
- 1 cup fresh spinach
- 1/2 cup crumbled feta cheese
- 1/4 cup sliced almonds
- 1 tbsp. olive oil
- 1 lemon, juiced
- Salt and pepper to taste

Instructions:

1. In a medium saucepan, bring the quinoa and water to a boil. Minimize the heat to a simmer and let the mixture cook for about 15-20 minutes.

2. Combine the cooked quinoa, sliced avocado, cherry tomatoes, fresh spinach, crumbled feta cheese, and sliced almonds in a large mixing bowl.
3. Pour a small amount of olive oil and lemon juice over the top, then add salt and pepper according to your preferences.
4. Divide the mixture into 4 bowls and serve.

Nutrition Information (per serving): Calories: 380 Fat: 22g Saturated Fat: 5g Cholesterol: 20mg Sodium: 350mg Carbohydrates: 36g Fiber: 9g Sugar: 3g Protein: 12g

CINNAMON ALMOND OATMEAL

Preparation time: 5 minutes
Cook time: 15 minutes
Servings: 2

Ingredients:

- 1 cup rolled oats
- 2 cups almond milk
- 2 tablespoons chia seeds
- 2 tablespoons maple syrup
- 1 teaspoon vanilla extract
- 1 teaspoon cinnamon
- 1/4 cup slivered almonds
- Fresh fruit for topping (optional)

Instructions:

1. Bring the almond milk to a boil over medium heat in a medium saucepan.
2. Stir in the oats, chia seeds, maple syrup, vanilla extract, and cinnamon.
3. Lower the heat to a low setting and continue cooking for approximately 10-15 minutes until the oats have become tender and the mixture has thickened.

4. Stir in the slivered almonds.
5. Serve in bowls and top with fresh fruit if desired.

Nutrition information (per serving): Calories: 333 Fat: 13g Carbohydrates: 50g Protein: 10g Fiber: 9g.

BERRY AND YOGURT PARFAIT

Preparation Time: 5 minutes
Cook Time: 0 minutes
Servings: 1-2

Ingredients:

- 1 cup fresh mixed berries (strawberries, blueberries, raspberries)
- 1 cup plain Greek yogurt
- 2 tablespoons chia seeds
- 1 teaspoon honey
- 1/4 teaspoon vanilla extract
- 1/4 teaspoon cinnamon

Instructions:

1. Mix the chia seeds, honey, vanilla extract, and cinnamon in a small bowl.
2. Layer the yogurt and the berry mixture in a tall glass or jar.
3. Sprinkle the chia seed mixture over the top.
4. Repeat the process of layering until all of the ingredients have been used.
5. You can serve the dish immediately or put it in the fridge to consume later.

Nutrition Information (per serving): Calories: 250 Fat: 9g Carbohydrates: 32g Protein: 15g

SPINACH AND FETA OMELETTE

Preparation time: 10 minutes
Cook time: 10 minutes
Servings: 1

Ingredients:

- 2 large eggs

- 1/4 cup packed baby spinach leaves

- 1/4 cup crumbled feta cheese

- 1 tsp olive oil

- Salt and pepper, to taste

Instructions:

1. Whisk the eggs in a medium bowl and add salt and pepper according to your preference.

2. Heat the olive oil in a non-stick frying pan over medium heat.

3. Add the baby spinach leaves to the pan and cook until wilted, about 2 minutes.

4. Over the spinach, pour the whisked eggs and sprinkle crumbled feta cheese on top.

5. Use a spatula to fold the omelet in half gently.

6. Cook until the eggs are set and the cheese is melted, about 5 minutes.

7. Serve hot, and enjoy!

Nutrition Info (per serving): Calories: 235 Fat: 18 g Carbohydrates: 4 g Protein: 16 g Sodium: 578 mg Sugar: 2 g

TOFU SCRAMBLE

Preparation time: 10 minutes
Cook time: 10 minutes
Servings: 2

Ingredients:

- 1 tablespoon olive oil
- 1 small onion, chopped
- 1 red bell pepper, chopped
- 1 garlic clove, minced
- 1 block of firm tofu, crumbled
- 1/4 teaspoon turmeric
- 1/4 teaspoon cumin
- Salt and pepper to taste
- 2 cups baby spinach
- 1 avocado, sliced
- 2 whole grain tortillas, warmed

Instructions:

1. Begin by warming the olive oil in a large skillet to medium heat.
2. Add the onion and red bell pepper and cook until softened, about 5-6 minutes.
3. Saute the garlic for a minute.
4. Add the crumbled tofu, turmeric, cumin, salt, and pepper to the skillet. Cook, frequently stirring, until the tofu is heated, about 5 minutes.
5. Stir in the baby spinach until wilted.
6. Serve the tofu scramble in a tortilla with sliced avocado.

Nutrition Information (per serving): Calories: 375 Fat: 26g Carbohydrates: 29g Protein: 16g Sodium: 590mg Fiber: 11g

EGG AND AVOCADO TOAST

Prep Time: 10 minutes
Cook Time: 10 minutes

Servings: 1

- Ingredients: 1 ripe avocado
- 1 large egg
- 1 slice of whole-grain bread
- 1 pinch of salt
- 1 pinch of black pepper
- 1 squeeze of lemon juice

Instructions:
1. Toast the slice of whole grain bread in a toaster or pan until golden brown.
2. Cut the avocado in half, remove the pit, and mash the avocado with a fork in a small bowl.
3. Season the mashed avocado with salt, black pepper, and lemon juice.

4. Fry the egg in a pan over medium heat until the whites are set and the yolks are still runny.
5. Spread the mashed avocado onto the toasted bread.
6. Place the fried egg on top of the avocado toast.
7. Serve hot, and enjoy!

Nutrition Information (per serving): Calories: 380 Fat: 26g Carbohydrates: 28g Protein: 13g Sodium: 470mg Fiber: 11g

BOWL WITH SWEET POTATO AND AVOCADO

Preparation Time: 10 minutes
Cook Time: 15 minutes
Servings: 1

Ingredients:

- 1 medium sweet potato, peeled and diced
- 1 ripe avocado, pitted and diced
- 1 tbsp olive oil
- 1/2 tsp sea salt
- 1/2 tsp black pepper
- 1/4 cup quinoa, cooked
- 1/4 cup cherry tomatoes, halved
- 1/4 cup sliced red onion
- 1/4 cup chopped fresh cilantro
- 1 tbsp lemon juice

Instructions:
1. Heat your oven to a temperature of 400°F (200°C).
2. Mix the diced sweet potato with olive oil, salt, and pepper on a baking sheet.
3. Roast for 15 minutes or until the sweet potato is tender and slightly golden.
4. Combine the cooked quinoa, cherry tomatoes, red onion, cilantro, and lemon juice in a medium bowl.
5. To serve, divide the quinoa mixture between two bowls.
6. Top each bowl with half of the roasted sweet potato and avocado.

Nutrition Information (per serving): Calories: 420 Fat: 28g Saturated Fat: 4g Carbohydrates: 43g Fiber: 9g Protein: 8g

TURMERIC OATMEAL BOWL

Preparation time: 5 minutes

Cook time: 5 minutes

Servings: 1

Ingredients:
- 1/2 cup rolled oats
- 1 cup water
- 1/2 teaspoon turmeric powder
- 1/2 teaspoon cinnamon
- 1/2 banana, sliced
- 1 tablespoon almond butter
- 1 tablespoon raisins
- 1 tablespoon chopped walnuts

Instructions:
1. Heat the water in a small saucepan until it comes to a boil.
2. Stir in the oats, turmeric, and cinnamon.
3. Lower the heat to a simmer and allow it to cook for 5 minutes, occasionally stirring until the oats are soft and the liquid has been absorbed.

4. Pour the oatmeal into a serving bowl.
5. Top with sliced banana, almond butter, raisins, and chopped walnuts.

Nutrition Information (per serving): Calories: 400 Fat: 18g Saturated Fat: 2g Carbohydrates: 56g Fiber: 7g Sugar: 15g Protein: 11g

AVOCADO TOAST WITH POACHED EGG

Preparation Time: 10 minutes
Cook Time: 10 minutes
Servings: 2

Ingredients:

- 2 slices of whole-grain bread
- 1 ripe avocado
- 2 eggs
- 1 tablespoon white wine vinegar
- Salt and pepper, to taste
- Two tablespoons of freshly chopped herbs, such as cilantro or parsley.

Instructions:

1. Toast the bread slices until golden and crispy.
2. Cut the avocado in half, remove the pit, and use a fork to mash the flesh. Spread the mashed avocado over the slices of toast.
3. Fill a medium saucepan with water and bring it to a simmer. Add the white wine vinegar and stir.
4. Crack an egg into a small bowl and gently pour it into the simmering water. Repeat with the second egg.

5. Cook the eggs for 3-4 minutes or until the whites are set and the yolks are still runny.
6. Use a slotted spoon to remove the eggs from the water and place them on top of the avocado toast.
7. Sprinkle salt, pepper, and chopped herbs over the eggs and serve immediately.

Nutrition Information (per serving): Calories: 324 Fat: 24g Saturated Fat: 4g Cholesterol: 186mg Sodium: 440mg Carbohydrates: 18g Fiber: 8g Sugar: 2g Protein: 12g

SPINACH, FETA, AND TOMATO OMELETTE

Preparation time: 10 minutes
Cook time: 10 minutes
Servings: 1

Ingredients:
- 2 large eggs
- 1/4 cup baby spinach
- 1 tablespoon crumbled feta cheese
- 1 tablespoon diced cherry tomatoes
- Salt and pepper, to taste
- 1 teaspoon olive oil

Instructions:
1. Crack the eggs into a bowl and beat them with a fork.
2. Heat the olive oil in a small skillet over medium heat.
3. Mix the spinach, feta cheese, and cherry tomatoes into the eggs.
4. Add the egg mixture to the skillet and cook for 2-3 minutes or until the bottom has become firm.

5. Fold the omelet in half using a spatula and cook for another 2-3 minutes or until the eggs are fully cooked.
6. Season with salt and pepper to taste.
7. Serve hot, and enjoy!

Nutrition information (per serving): Calories: 200 Fat: 15g Protein: 13g Carbohydrates: 5g Sodium: 400mg

TURMERIC QUINOA PORRIDGE

Preparation Time: 10 minutes
Cook Time: 15 minutes
Servings: 2

Ingredients:

- 1 cup quinoa
- 2 cups water
- 1 tsp turmeric powder
- 1/2 tsp cinnamon powder
- 1/4 tsp ground ginger
- 1 tbsp maple syrup
- 1 cup almond milk
- 1/2 cup mixed berries
- 1 tbsp chopped almonds
- 1 tsp coconut oil

Instructions:

1. Rinse the quinoa thoroughly in a fine mesh strainer and set aside.

2. Add the quinoa, water, turmeric, cinnamon, ginger, and maple syrup in a medium saucepan.
3. Heat the mixture until it comes to a boil, and then lower the heat to a simmer.
4. Cover the saucepan and cook for 15 minutes or until the quinoa is tender and the water is absorbed.
5. Stir in the almond milk and heat the mixture for a minute or two.
6. In a small pan, heat the coconut oil and add the mixed berries. Cook for 2-3 minutes or until the berries are soft.
7. Serve the quinoa porridge in a bowl and top with the berry mixture, chopped almonds, and an extra drizzle of maple syrup if desired.

Nutrition Information (per serving): Calories: 337 Fat: 12g Protein: 11g Carbohydrates: 52g Sugar: 16g Fiber: 7g

SPICED SWEET POTATO HASH

Preparation Time: 10 minutes
Cook Time: 20 minutes
Servings: 4

Ingredients:

- 2 medium sweet potatoes, peeled and diced
- 1 small red onion, diced
- 1 red bell pepper, diced
- 1 teaspoon ground cumin
- 1 teaspoon chili powder
- 1/2 teaspoon smoked paprika
- 1/4 teaspoon sea salt
- 2 tablespoons olive oil
- 4 large eggs

Instructions:

1. Preheat your air fryer to 400°F.

2. Mix the diced sweet potatoes, red onion, and bell pepper in a large bowl.
3. Add the spices, salt, and olive oil to the bowl and toss until the vegetables are evenly coated.
4. Place the mixture in the air fryer basket and cook for 20 minutes, stirring occasionally, until the vegetables are tender and slightly crispy.
5. While the hash is cooking, fry the eggs in a non-stick pan to your desired level of doneness.
6. Serve the sweet potato hash topped with the fried eggs. Enjoy!

Nutrition Info (per serving): Calories: 220 Fat: 9g Carbohydrates: 31g Protein: 4g Fiber: 5g

TOMATO, FETA, AND AVOCADO TOAST

Preparation Time: 10 minutes
Cook Time: 5 minutes
Servings: 1

Ingredients:

- 1 slice of whole-grain bread
- 1 ripe avocado
- 1 medium tomato
- 1 oz feta cheese
- Salt and pepper, to taste
- 1 tsp olive oil

Instructions:

1. Toast the slice of whole grain bread until golden brown.
2. Cut the avocado in half and remove the pit. Mash one-half of the avocado on the toast.
3. Slice the tomato and place it on top of the mashed avocado.
4. Crumble the feta cheese over the tomato.
5. Add a drizzle of olive oil and salt and pepper to taste.

6. Serve immediately and enjoy.

Nutrition Information (per serving): Calories: 376 Fat: 28g Carbohydrates: 27g Protein: 9g Sodium: 499mg Fiber: 8g

SPINACH AND FETA BREAKFAST BAKE

Preparation Time: 10 minutes
Cook Time: 30 minutes
Servings: 4

Ingredients:

- 1 cup quinoa, rinsed and drained
- 2 cups vegetable broth
- 1 cup cherry tomatoes, halved
- 1 cup fresh spinach, chopped
- 4 large eggs
- 1/2 cup crumbled feta cheese
- 1/4 cup diced red onion
- 2 cloves garlic, minced
- Salt and pepper to taste
- 1 tbsp. olive oil

Instructions:

1. Preheat oven to 375°F.

2. Bring the vegetable broth and quinoa to a boil in a medium-sized saucepan. Once boiling, lower the heat, cover the pan, and let it simmer for approximately 20 minutes or until the quinoa becomes tender and the liquid is fully absorbed.
3. Using a large bowl, beat the eggs until thoroughly combined. Add the cooked quinoa, cherry tomatoes, spinach, feta cheese, red onion, garlic, salt, and pepper. Mix well.
4. In a 9x9 inch baking dish, drizzle the olive oil to coat the bottom. Next, pour the egg mixture into the dish.
5. Place this in the oven and bake for approximately 30 minutes or until the eggs have solidified and the top has become lightly golden brown.
6. Serve hot, and enjoy!

Nutrition Info (per serving): Calories: 300 Fat: 15g Carbohydrates: 25g Protein: 15g

SPICED OATMEAL WITH FRESH BERRIES

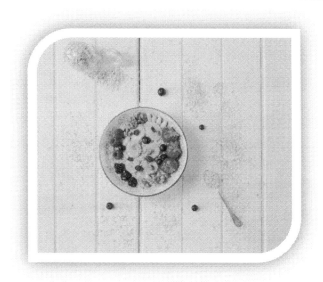

Preparation Time: 5 minutes
Cook Time: 15 minutes
Servings: 2

Ingredients:

- 1 cup rolled oats
- 1 1/2 cups water
- 1/2 teaspoon ground cinnamon
- 1/4 teaspoon ground nutmeg
- 1/4 teaspoon ground ginger
- 1/4 teaspoon salt
- 1/4 cup almond milk
- 1/4 cup maple syrup
- 1 cup mixed fresh berries (such as strawberries, raspberries, and blueberries)
- 1/4 cup chopped almonds

Instructions:

1. Combine the oats, water, cinnamon, nutmeg, ginger, and salt in a medium saucepan. Bring to a boil over medium heat.

2. Reduce the heat to low and cook, occasionally stirring, for 10-12 minutes or until the oats are tender and the liquid is absorbed.
3. Stir in the almond milk and maple syrup.
4. Separate the oatmeal into two serving bowls, then add an equal amount of mixed berries and chopped almonds to each bowl.

Nutrition Information: Calories: 380 Fat: 9g Saturated Fat: 1g Cholesterol: 0mg Sodium: 330mg Carbohydrates: 71g Fiber: 7g Sugar: 28g Protein: 10g

TURMERIC CHIA SEED PUDDING

Preparation Time: 10 minutes

Cook Time: None

Servings: 2

Ingredients:

- 1 cup almond milk
- 1/4 cup chia seeds
- 1 tsp turmeric powder
- 1 tsp vanilla extract
- 1 tbsp honey
- Fresh berries for serving
- Sliced almonds for garnish

Instructions:

1. In a medium bowl, whisk the almond milk, chia seeds, turmeric powder, vanilla extract, and honey until well combined.
2. Once you've covered the bowl, put it in the refrigerator for at least 2 hours or overnight.

3. Divide the pudding into two serving glasses and top with fresh berries and sliced almonds.

Nutrition Information per serving: Calories: 250 Fat: 13g Saturated Fat: 1g Cholesterol: 0mg Sodium: 140mg Carbohydrates: 28g Fiber: 9g Sugar: 17g Protein: 8g

BLUEBERRY AND ALMOND BUTTER TOAST

Preparation time: 5 minutes

Cook time: 2 minutes

Servings: 2

Ingredients:

- 2 slices of whole-grain bread
- 2 tablespoons of almond butter
- 1/2 cup of fresh blueberries
- 1 teaspoon of honey
- 1/4 teaspoon of cinnamon
- A pinch of salt

Instructions:

1. Toast the slices of whole grain bread in a toaster until they are crispy and golden brown.
2. Spread 1 tablespoon of almond butter on each slice of toast.
3. Top the almond butter with fresh blueberries.
4. Drizzle 1/2 teaspoon of honey over each slice of toast.
5. Sprinkle 1/4 teaspoon of cinnamon and a pinch of salt over each slice.
6. Serve immediately and enjoy your healthy and delicious breakfast.

Nutrition Information: Calories: 357 Fat: 21g Saturated Fat: 2g Cholesterol: 0mg Sodium: 235mg Carbohydrates: 38g Fiber: 5g Sugar: 18g Protein: 9g

SNACKS

SPICED CHICKPEAS SNACK RECIPE

Preparation time: 10 minutes

Cook time: 40 minutes

Servings: 4

Ingredients:

- 1 can of chickpeas (15 ounces), drained and rinsed
- 1 tablespoon of olive oil
- 1 teaspoon of cumin
- 1 teaspoon of paprika
- 1/2 teaspoon of chili powder
- 1/2 teaspoon of garlic powder
- 1/2 teaspoon of salt
- 1/4 teaspoon of black pepper

Instructions:

1. Heat your oven in advance to a temperature of 400°F (200°C).
2. Mix chickpeas with olive oil, cumin, paprika, chili powder, garlic powder, salt, and pepper until all ingredients are well combined.

3. Arrange the chickpeas on a baking sheet, spreading them out in a single, even layer.
4. Bake in the oven for 40 minutes, occasionally stirring, until the chickpeas are crispy and golden brown.
5. Serve as a snack or sprinkle over a salad for extra crunch.

Nutrition Information (per serving): Calories: 150 Fat: 7g Saturated Fat: 1g Cholesterol: 0mg Sodium: 420mg Carbohydrates: 20g Fiber: 5g Sugar: 2g Protein: 6g

CHERRY TOMATO AND BASIL BRUSCHETTA

Preparation time: 10 minutes
Cook time: 5 minutes
Servings: 4

Ingredients:

- 8 slices of whole grain bread
- 1-pint cherry tomatoes halved
- 1/4 cup fresh basil leaves, chopped
- 2 cloves garlic, minced
- 2 tbsp. extra-virgin olive oil
- Salt and pepper to taste

Instructions:

1. Preheat the oven to 400°F.
2. Toast the bread slices until golden brown.
3. Mix the cherry tomatoes, basil, garlic, olive oil, salt, and pepper in a bowl.
4. Spoon the tomato mixture over the toasted bread slices.
5. Bake in the oven for 5 minutes or until the bread is crispy and the tomato mixture is heated.

6. Serve hot.

Nutrition Information (per serving): Calories: 190 Fat: 9g Saturated Fat: 1.5g Cholesterol: 0mg Sodium: 300mg Carbohydrates: 25g Fiber: 3g Sugar: 3g Protein: 5g

SPICY ROASTED CHICKPEAS

Preparation Time: 5 minutes
Cook Time: 20-25 minutes
Servings: 4

Ingredients:

- 1 can chickpeas, drained and rinsed
- 1 tablespoon olive oil
- 1 teaspoon chili powder
- 1 teaspoon cumin
- 1/2 teaspoon paprika
- 1/2 teaspoon garlic powder
- Salt and pepper to taste

Instructions:

1. Preheat the oven to 400°F. Line a baking sheet with parchment paper.
2. Mix olive oil, chili powder, cumin, paprika, garlic powder, salt, and pepper with the chickpeas in a medium-sized bowl.
3. Arrange the chickpeas on the baking sheet, spreading them in a single layer.
4. Bake for 20-25 minutes or until crispy and golden brown.
5. Serve immediately.

Nutrition Information: Calories: 150 Fat: 7g Saturated Fat: 1g Cholesterol: 0mg Sodium: 200mg Carbohydrates: 19g Fiber: 5g Sugar: 2g Protein: 6g

SPICY BAKED SWEET POTATO CHIPS

Preparation Time: 10 minutes
Cook Time: 25 minutes
Servings: 4

Ingredients:

- 4 medium sweet potatoes, sliced thin
- 1 tablespoon olive oil
- 1 teaspoon chili powder
- 1 teaspoon paprika
- 1/2 teaspoon garlic powder
- Salt and pepper to taste

Instructions:

1. Heat your oven to a temperature of 400°F (200°C) and cover a baking sheet with parchment paper.
2. Mix the sliced sweet potatoes, olive oil, chili powder, paprika, garlic powder, salt, and pepper in a large bowl.
3. Place the sweet potato slices on the prepared baking sheet, spreading them in a single, even layer.
4. Bake for 25 minutes, flipping the slices halfway through or until the sweet potatoes are crispy and lightly browned.
5. Serve immediately.

Nutrition Information (per serving): Calories: 140 Fat: 5g Saturated Fat: 1g Cholesterol: 0mg Sodium: 120mg Carbohydrates: 24g Fiber: 4g Sugr: 6g Protein: 2g

TURMERIC AND GINGER OATMEAL BOWL

Preparation time: 10 minutes

Cook time: 10 minutes

Servings: 2

Ingredients:

- 1 cup of old-fashioned oats
- 2 cups of water
- 1 tsp turmeric powder
- 1 tsp freshly grated ginger
- 1 tbsp honey
- 1 tbsp olive oil
- 1 tsp cinnamon
- 1 cup of mixed berries
- 1/4 cup of almonds, chopped

Instructions:

1. Heat the water in a medium-sized saucepan until it boils.
2. Add the oats to the mixture and reduce the heat to a low temperature. Stir the mixture occasionally and allow it to cook for 5 minutes.

3. Put turmeric, ginger, honey, olive oil, and cinnamon into the oatmeal.
4. Cook for 5 minutes or until the oatmeal is thick and creamy.
5. Divide the oatmeal into two serving bowls and top with mixed berries and chopped almonds.
6. Serve immediately and enjoy.

Nutrition Information: Calories: 438 Fat: 17g Saturated Fat: 2g Cholesterol: 0mg Sodium: 11mg Carbohydrates: 67g Fiber: 7g Sugar: 26g Protein: 10g

ALMOND BUTTER BANANA OATMEAL

Preparation Time: 5 minutes

Cook Time: 10 minutes

Servings: 2

Ingredients:

- 1 cup rolled oats
- 2 ripe bananas, mashed
- 2 cups almond milk
- 2 tablespoons almond butter
- 1 teaspoon cinnamon
- 1/4 teaspoon salt
- Fresh berries and honey for serving (optional)

Instructions:

1. Combine the oats, mashed bananas, almond milk, butter, cinnamon, and salt in a medium saucepan.

2. Stir constantly while cooking over medium heat for 10 minutes or until the oatmeal has become creamy and the desired texture is achieved.
3. Serve the oatmeal hot with fresh berries and a drizzle of honey, if desired.

Nutrition Information (per serving): Calories: 420 Fat: 18g Saturated Fat: 2g Cholesterol: 0mg Sodium: 340mg Carbohydrates: 63g Fiber: 10g Sugar: 19g Protein: 11g

SPICY QUINOA STUFFED BELL PEPPERS RECIPE

Preparation time: 20 minutes

Cook time: 30 minutes

Servings: 4

Ingredients:

- 4 large bell peppers (red, yellow, or green)
- 1 cup quinoa, cooked
- One can of black beans has been drained and rinsed.
- 1/2 cup corn kernels
- 1/2 red onion, chopped
- 1 jalapeno, seeded and minced
- 1 clove of garlic, minced
- 1 tsp chili powder
- 1 tsp ground cumin
- 1 tsp paprika

- 1/4 tsp salt
- 1/4 tsp black pepper
- 1/2 cup salsa
- 1/2 cup shredded cheddar cheese
- Fresh cilantro, chopped for garnish

Instructions:
1. Heat your oven in advance to a temperature of 375°F.
2. Remove the tops of the bell peppers and take out the seeds.
3. Mix the cooked quinoa, black beans, corn, red onion, jalapeno, garlic, chili powder, cumin, paprika, salt, and pepper in a large bowl.
4. Stuff the mixture into the hollowed-out bell peppers.
5. Put the stuffed bell peppers in a baking dish.
6. Pour the salsa over the stuffed bell peppers.
7. Sprinkle shredded cheddar cheese over the salsa.
8. Place the baking dish inside the oven and cook for 25-30 minutes, or until the bell peppers have become tender and the cheese has melted.
9. Garnish with fresh cilantro and serve hot.

Nutrition Information (per serving): Calories: 330 Fat: 9g Saturated Fat: 4g Cholesterol: 20mg Sodium: 570mg Carbohydrates: 50g Fiber: 8g Sugar: 8g Protein: 15g

PESTO CHICKEN WITH ROASTED TOMATOES AND ASPARAGUS

Preparation Time: 10 minutes
Cook Time: 30 minutes
Servings: 4

Ingredients:

- 4 boneless, skinless chicken breasts
- 1/2 cup basil pesto
- 4 tablespoons olive oil, divided
- 1-pint cherry tomatoes
- 1 pound asparagus, trimmed
- Salt and pepper to taste

Instructions:

1. Preheat the oven to 400°F.
2. Put the chicken breasts into a baking dish without copying the original sentence in an orderly manner and spread 2 tablespoons of pesto evenly over each one.
3. In a separate baking dish, toss the cherry tomatoes and asparagus with 2 tablespoons of olive oil and season with salt and pepper.
4. Bake the chicken and vegetables for 25-30 minutes or until the chicken is tender.

5. Serve the chicken with roasted tomatoes and asparagus on the side.

Nutrition Information: Calories: 460 Fat: 36g Saturated Fat: 7g Cholesterol: 93mg Sodium: 582mg Carbohydrates: 9g Fiber: 3g Sugar: 4g Protein: 33g

LEMON & HERB GRILLED CHICKEN WITH QUINOA & BROCCOLI

Preparation Time: 15 minutes
Cook Time: 25 minutes
Servings: 4

Ingredients:

- 4 boneless, skinless chicken breasts
- 2 lemons, juiced
- 2 tbsp. olive oil
- 2 cloves of garlic, minced
- 2 tsp. dried basil
- 1 tsp. dried thyme
- 1 tsp. dried rosemary
- Salt and pepper, to taste
- 1 cup quinoa
- 2 cups water
- 4 cups broccoli florets

Instructions:

1. Combine lemon juice, olive oil, garlic, basil, thyme, rosemary, pepper, and salt in a small bowl and mix them well.
2. Set the chicken in a shallow dish and pour the lemon mixture over the chicken, making sure it is evenly coated.
3. In a separate pot, bring quinoa and water to a simmer. Minimize heat to low, cover, and let simmer for 15-20 minutes or until the water is absorbed.
4. While the quinoa is cooking, heat a grill or grill pan to medium-high heat.
5. Set chicken on the grill and cook for 5-7 minutes on each side or until fully cooked.
6. In a separate pan, steam broccoli for 5-7 minutes or until tender.
7. Serve chicken with quinoa and steamed broccoli on the side.

Nutrition Information: Calories: 380 Fat: 11g Saturated Fat: 2g Cholesterol: 73mg Sodium: 119mg Carbohydrates: 36g Fiber: 5g Sugar: 2g Protein: 35g

SPICED LENTIL AND VEGETABLE STEW

Preparation Time: 15 minutes
Cook Time: 40 minutes
Servings: 4

Ingredients:

- 1 tablespoon olive oil
- 1 onion, chopped
- 2 cloves garlic, minced
- 1 teaspoon ground cumin
- 1 teaspoon ground coriander
- 1/2 teaspoon turmeric
- 1/2 teaspoon paprika
- 1 can (14.5 oz) diced tomatoes
- 1 cup green lentils, rinsed and drained
- 4 cups vegetable broth
- 2 carrots, peeled and chopped
- 2 stalks of celery, chopped
- 1 zucchini, chopped
- Salt and pepper, to taste

- Fresh cilantro for garnish

Instructions:
1. Place a large saucepan on medium heat and heat the oil.
2. Add the onion to the saucepan and cook for 3 minutes, until softened.
3. Add the garlic, cumin, coriander, turmeric, and paprika and cook for 1 minute, until fragrant.
4. Add the diced tomatoes, lentils, vegetable broth, carrots, celery, and zucchini to the saucepan.
5. Mix the ingredients and heat until boiling.
6. Lower the heat to a low setting, cover the saucepan, and let it simmer for 30-35 minutes or until the lentils and vegetables are tender.
7. Season with salt and pepper to taste.
8. Serve hot, garnished with fresh cilantro.

Nutrition Information (per serving): Calories: 250 Fat: 6g Saturated Fat: 1g Cholesterol: 0mg Sodium: 800mg Carbohydrates: 39g Fiber: 13g Sugar: 9g Protein: 12g

LEMON AND HERB GRILLED SALMON

Preparation Time: 10 minutes
Cook Time: 12 minutes
Servings: 4

Ingredients:

- 4 salmon fillets, about 6 oz each
- 3 tbsp olive oil
- 1 lemon, zested and juiced
- 2 garlic cloves, minced
- 2 tbsp fresh basil, chopped
- 2 tbsp fresh parsley, chopped
- 1 tsp salt
- 1/2 tsp black pepper

Instructions:

1. Preheat your grill to high heat.

2. Whisk the olive oil, lemon juice and zest, garlic, basil, parsley, salt, and pepper in a small mixing bowl.
3. Put the salmon fillets in a dish that is not deep, and spread the marinade on the salmon, ensuring that each fillet is covered equally.
4. Allow the salmon to marinate for 5 minutes.
5. Grill the salmon fillets over high heat for 6 minutes on each side or until the internal temperature reaches 140°F.
6. Serve the grilled salmon hot with fresh lemon juice and chopped herbs.

Nutrition Information (per serving): Calories: 350 Fat: 23g Saturated Fat: 3g Cholesterol: 93mg Sodium: 550mg Carbohydrates: 2g Fiber: 1g Sugar: 1g Protein: 36g

LEMON AND HERB GRILLED CHICKEN

Preparation Time: 10 minutes

Cook Time: 20 minutes

Servings: 4

Ingredients:

- 4 boneless, skinless chicken breasts
- 2 tablespoons olive oil
- 2 cloves garlic, minced
- 1 lemon, juiced
- 1 teaspoon dried basil
- 1 teaspoon dried oregano
- 1 teaspoon dried thyme
- Salt and pepper, to taste

Instructions:

1. Mix the olive oil, garlic, lemon juice, basil, oregano, thyme, salt, and pepper in a large bowl.
2. Add the chicken breasts to the marinade and sit in the refrigerator for at least 30 minutes or up to 2 hours.
3. Preheat the grill to medium-high heat.

4. Remove the chicken from the marinade and grill for 10 minutes on each side or until the internal temperature reaches 165°F.
5. Serve with a side of roasted vegetables and a lemon wedge.

Nutrition Information (per serving): Calories: 251 Fat: 14g Saturated Fat: 2g Cholesterol: 72mg Sodium: 212mg Carbohydrates: 2g Fiber: 1g Sugar: 1g Protein: 27g

GRILLED SALMON WITH ROASTED VEGETABLES

Preparation time: 15 minutes

Cook time: 20 minutes

Servings: 4

Ingredients:

- 4 salmon fillets, 6 ounces each
- 1 red bell pepper, sliced
- 1 yellow onion, sliced
- 1 zucchini, sliced
- 1 eggplant, sliced
- 4 garlic cloves, minced
- 1/4 cup olive oil
- Salt and pepper to taste

Instructions:

1. Preheat the grill to medium-high heat.
2. Mix the red bell pepper, yellow onion, zucchini, eggplant, garlic, olive oil, salt, and pepper in a large bowl.

3. Place the vegetables on the grill, and cook for 10 minutes or until tender and slightly charred.
4. Place the salmon fillets on the grill and cook for 10 minutes or until the salmon is cooked through and flaky.
5. Serve the grilled salmon with the roasted vegetables.

Nutrition Information (per serving): Calories: 380 Fat: 24g Saturated Fat: 4g Cholesterol: 72mg Sodium: 175mg Carbohydrates: 14g Fiber: 4g Sugar: 5g Protein: 33g

ROASTED SALMON WITH QUINOA AND VEGETABLES

Preparation Time: 10 minutes
Cook Time: 20 minutes
Servings: 4

Ingredients:

- 4 salmon fillets
- 2 tablespoons of olive oil
- Salt and pepper to taste
- 1 cup of quinoa
- 2 cups of water
- 2 cups of mixed vegetables (such as bell peppers, carrots, and zucchini)
- 2 cloves of garlic, minced

Instructions:

1. Preheat your oven to 400°F (200°C).
2. Line a baking sheet with parchment paper.
3. Rinse the quinoa and place it in a medium saucepan with water. Bring the water to a boil, reduce the heat to low, cover the saucepan, and let the quinoa cook for 15 minutes or until tender.

4. While the quinoa is cooking, prepare the vegetables by cutting them into bite-sized pieces.
5. Toss the vegetables with olive oil, minced garlic, salt, and pepper in a large mixing bowl.
6. Place the salmon fillets on one-half of the prepared baking sheet.
7. Arrange the seasoned vegetables on the other half of the baking sheet.
8. Bake in the oven for 20 minutes or until the salmon is cooked and the vegetables are tender.
9. Serve the salmon with a bed of cooked quinoa and roasted vegetables on the side.

Nutrition Information (per serving): Calories: 420 Fat: 20g Saturated Fat: 3g Cholesterol: 65mg Sodium: 120mg Carbohydrates: 28g Fiber: 4g Sugar: 4g Protein: 36g

GRILLED SALMON WITH AVOCADO SALSA

Preparation Time: 15 minutes

Cook Time: 12 minutes

Servings: 4

Ingredients:

- 4 salmon fillets
- 1 avocado, diced
- 1 large tomato, diced
- 1/2 red onion, diced
- 1 jalapeno, seeded and diced
- 1 lime, juiced
- Salt and pepper to taste

Instructions:

1. Preheat the grill to high heat.
2. Season salmon fillets with salt and pepper.
3. Combine diced avocado, tomato, red onion, jalapeno, and lime juice in a medium mixing bowl.

4. Place salmon fillets on the grill and cook for 6 minutes on each side or until fully cooked.
5. Serve salmon with avocado salsa on top.

Nutrition Information: Calories: 365 Fat: 25g Saturated Fat: 4g Cholesterol: 93mg Sodium: 121mg Carbohydrates: 8g Fiber: 4g Sugar: 3g Protein: 31g

SPICY TOFU STIR-FRY

Preparation Time: 10 minutes
Cook Time: 20 minutes
Servings: 4

Ingredients:

- 1 block of firm tofu, drained and cut into cubes
- 1 red bell pepper, sliced
- 1 yellow onion, sliced
- 1 zucchini, sliced
- 1 teaspoon chili flakes
- 2 tablespoons olive oil
- Salt and pepper, to taste
- 1 tablespoon soy sauce
- 2 teaspoons honey
- 2 cloves of garlic, minced
- 2 tablespoons sesame seeds
- Fresh cilantro for garnish

Instructions:
1. Mix soy sauce, honey, and minced garlic in a small bowl.
2. In a large skillet, heat the olive oil over medium heat.
3. Add the tofu and cook until browned, about 5-7 minutes.
4. Add the red bell pepper, yellow onion, and zucchini to the skillet. Cook for another 5-7 minutes until the vegetables are tender.
5. Stir in the chili flakes and the soy sauce mixture. Cook for 2-3 minutes, until the sauce has thickened.
6. Remove from heat and stir in the sesame seeds.
7. Serve over brown rice and garnish with fresh cilantro.

Nutrition Information: Calories: 256 Fat: 17g Saturated Fat: 2g Cholesterol: 0mg Sodium: 708mg Carbohydrates: 17g Fiber: 4g Sugar: 8g Protein: 11g

SPICY SHRIMP AND QUINOA BOWLS

Prep time: 10 minutes
Cook time: 20 minutes
Servings: 4

Ingredients:

- 1 cup of quinoa
- 2 tbsp olive oil
- 1 lb large shrimp, peeled and deveined
- 1 red bell pepper, diced
- 1 yellow onion, diced
- 3 cloves garlic, minced
- 1 tsp red pepper flakes
- 1 tsp smoked paprika
- 1 tsp ground cumin
- 1 tsp dried oregano
- Salt and pepper, to taste
- 2 tbsp lemon juice
- 1 avocado, diced
- Fresh cilantro for garnish

Instructions:
1. Cook the quinoa according to package instructions.
2. In a large skillet, heat the olive oil over medium heat. Add the shrimp and cook until they turn pink, about 2-3 minutes. Remove the shrimp from the skillet and set aside.
3. Add the red bell pepper, yellow onion, and garlic to the same skillet. Cook until the vegetables are soft and fragrant, about 5 minutes.
4. Add the red pepper flakes, smoked paprika, ground cumin, dried oregano, salt, and pepper to the skillet. Stir to combine.
5. Add the cooked shrimp to the skillet and pour in the lemon juice. Cook for an additional 2-3 minutes.
6. Serve the spicy shrimp and vegetable mixture over a bed of cooked quinoa. Top with diced avocado and fresh cilantro for garnish.

Nutrition Information (per serving): Calories: 420 Fat: 18g Saturated Fat: 3g Cholesterol: 215mg Sodium: 550mg Carbohydrates: 36g Fiber: 5g Sugar: 5g Protein: 32g

ROASTED SALMON WITH QUINOA AND BROCCOLI

Prep Time: 10 minutes
Cook Time: 25 minutes
Servings: 4

Ingredients:

- 4 salmon fillets (6 oz each)
- 1 cup quinoa
- 2 cups broccoli florets
- 1 tbsp olive oil
- Salt and pepper to taste
- 1 lemon, sliced
- 2 cloves of garlic, minced
- 2 tbsp balsamic vinegar

Instructions:

1. Preheat the oven to 400°F.
2. Prepare the quinoa by following the instructions on the packaging.
3. In a large mixing bowl, combine the broccoli florets, olive oil, salt, pepper, garlic, and balsamic vinegar. Toss until the broccoli is well coated.

4. Place the salmon fillets in a single layer on a baking sheet and top with lemon slices.
5. Roast the salmon for 20-25 minutes or until the internal temperature reaches 145°F.
6. Serve the roasted salmon over a bed of quinoa, topped with roasted broccoli.

Nutrition Information (per serving): Calories: 430 Fat: 19g Saturated Fat: 3g Cholesterol: 75mg Sodium: 330mg Carbohydrates: 32g Fiber: 4g Sugar: 5g Protein: 37g

ROASTED SALMON WITH CITRUS SALSA

Preparation time: 15 minutes
Cook time: 20 minutes
Servings: 4

Ingredients:

- 4 salmon fillets (6 oz each)
- Salt and pepper, to taste
- 1 tbsp olive oil
- 1 red onion, finely diced
- 2 oranges, peeled and chopped
- 2 limes, juiced
- 1 tbsp honey
- 1 tbsp chopped fresh cilantro

Instructions:

1. Set your oven to 400°F before starting to cook.
2. Sprinkle salt and pepper over the salmon fillets.

3. Heat the olive oil in a large oven-safe skillet over medium heat. Add the salmon fillets to the skillet, skin-side down, and cook for 2-3 minutes, until the skin is crispy.
4. Transfer the skillet to the oven and bake for 15-20 minutes until the salmon is cooked.
5. While the salmon is cooking, make the salsa by combining the red onion, chopped oranges, lime juice, honey, and cilantro in a bowl.
6. Serve the salmon with the citrus salsa on top.

Nutrition Information (per serving): Calories: 348 Fat: 22g Saturated Fat: 3g Cholesterol: 93mg Sodium: 146mg Carbohydrates: 18g Fiber: 4g Sugar: 13g Protein: 26g

ROASTED SALMON WITH AVOCADO SALSA

Preparation Time: 15 minutes

Cook Time: 20 minutes

Servings: 4

Ingredients:

- 4 salmon fillets
- 1 tsp. extra-virgin olive oil
- Salt and pepper to taste
- 1 ripe avocado, diced
- 1/2 red onion, finely chopped
- 1 large tomato, diced
- 2 tbsp. fresh cilantro, chopped
- 1 tsp. fresh lime juice
- 1 tsp. honey

Instructions:

1. Heat your oven to a temperature of 400°F (200°C) and cover a baking sheet with parchment paper.

2. Place the salmon fillets on the prepared baking sheet. Brush each fillet with olive oil and season with salt and pepper.
3. Roast the salmon in the oven for 20 minutes or until it is cooked.
4. While the salmon is cooking, make the avocado salsa. Mix the diced avocado, red onion, tomato, cilantro, lime juice, and honey in a medium bowl. Season with salt and pepper to taste.
5. Serve the roasted salmon with the avocado salsa on top.

Nutrition Information per Serving: Calories: 250 Fat: 15g Saturated Fat: 2g Cholesterol: 60mg Sodium: 160mg Carbohydrates: 10g Fiber: 4g Sugar: 5g Protein: 22g

ROASTED CAULIFLOWER AND CARROTS WITH TURMERIC AND GINGER

Preparation time: 10 minutes

Cook time: 25 minutes

Servings: 4

Ingredients:

- 1 head of cauliflower, chopped into florets
- 4 carrots, sliced into rounds
- 2 tablespoons olive oil
- 1 teaspoon turmeric powder
- 1 teaspoon ginger powder
- Salt and pepper to taste

Instructions:

1. Preheat the oven to 400°F (200°C).
2. Combine the chopped cauliflower, sliced carrots, olive oil, turmeric powder, ginger powder, salt, and pepper in a large mixing bowl.
3. Toss the ingredients together until the vegetables are evenly coated.
4. Spread the mixture out in a single layer on a baking sheet.
5. Bake for 25 minutes or until the vegetables are tender and golden brown.

6. Serve hot as a side dish.

Nutrition Information (per serving): Calories: 140 Fat: 10g Saturated Fat: 1.5g Cholesterol: 0mg Sodium: 150mg Carbohydrates: 12g Fiber: 5g Sugar: 5g Protein: 4g

ROASTED CAULIFLOWER WITH TURMERIC AND GARLIC

Preparation Time: 10 minutes
Cook Time: 25 minutes
Servings: 4

Ingredients:

- 1 head of cauliflower, cut into florets
- 3 cloves of garlic, minced
- 1 teaspoon of turmeric
- 2 tablespoons of olive oil
- Salt and pepper to taste

Instructions:

1. Preheat your oven to 400°F (200°C).
2. Combine the cauliflower florets, minced garlic, turmeric, olive oil, salt, and pepper in a large mixing bowl.
3. Toss everything together until the cauliflower is evenly coated with the seasonings.
4. Transfer the cauliflower to a baking sheet and bake in the oven for 25 minutes or until the florets are tender and slightly browned.

5. Serve hot as a side dish.

Nutrition Information per serving:

- Calories: 130
- Fat: 11g
- Saturated Fat: 1.5g
- Cholesterol: 0mg
- Sodium: 140mg
- Carbohydrates: 9g
- Fiber: 4g
- Sugar: 3g
- Protein: 4g

ROASTED GARLIC AND HERB QUINOA

Preparation time: 10 minutes

Cook time: 20 minutes

Servings: 4

Ingredients:

- 1 cup quinoa, rinsed
- 2 cups vegetable broth
- 4 cloves of garlic, minced
- 1 teaspoon dried thyme
- 1 teaspoon dried rosemary
- 1 teaspoon dried basil
- 1 tablespoon olive oil
- Salt and pepper to taste

Instructions:

1. Preheat your oven to 375°F.
2. In a medium saucepan, bring the vegetable broth to a boil. Add the rinsed quinoa and reduce heat to low. Cover and simmer for 18-20 minutes or until the liquid has been absorbed.

3. While the quinoa is cooking, mix the minced garlic with the dried herbs, olive oil, salt, and pepper in a small bowl.
4. Once the quinoa has finished cooking, transfer it to a 9x13-inch baking dish. Spread the garlic and herb mixture evenly over the top of the quinoa.
5. Bake in the oven for 10-12 minutes or until the garlic is fragrant and the quinoa is lightly toasted.
6. Serve hot as a side dish.

Nutrition Information (per serving): Calories: 199 Fat: 7g Saturated Fat: 1g Cholesterol: 0mg Sodium: 556mg Carbohydrates: 28g Fiber: 3g Sugar: 1g Protein: 7g

GRILLED ASPARAGUS WITH LEMON AND PARMESAN

Preparation time: 10 minutes
Cook time: 10 minutes
Servings: 4

Ingredients:

- 1 lb asparagus, trimmed
- 2 tbsp olive oil
- Salt and pepper to taste
- 1 lemon, juiced
- 1/4 cup grated parmesan cheese

Instructions:

1. Preheat your grill to medium-high heat.

2. Toss the asparagus with olive oil, salt, and pepper in a large mixing bowl.
3. Place the asparagus on the grill and cook for 8-10 minutes, occasionally turning, until tender and charred.
4. Remove the asparagus from the grill and place it in a serving dish.
5. Drizzle the lemon juice over the asparagus and sprinkle it with parmesan cheese.
6. Serve hot, and enjoy!

Nutrition Information: Calories: 150 Fat: 13g Saturated Fat: 3g Cholesterol: 5mg Sodium: 200mg Carbohydrates: 8g Fiber: 3g Sugar: 3g Protein: 6g

ROASTED CARROT AND FENNEL SIDE DISH

Preparation Time: 15 minutes

Cook Time: 30 minutes

Servings: 4

Ingredients:

- 1 lb. carrots, peeled and chopped
- 1 medium fennel bulb, chopped
- 1 tbsp. olive oil
- 1 tsp. dried thyme
- 1 tsp. dried rosemary
- Salt and pepper to taste

Instructions:

1. Preheat the oven to 400°F (200°C).
2. In a large mixing bowl, combine the chopped carrots and fennel.
3. Add the olive oil, thyme, rosemary, salt, and pepper to the bowl and mix well to coat the vegetables evenly.
4. Transfer the mixture to a baking sheet and spread it into a single layer.
5. Bake for 30 minutes or until the vegetables are tender and golden brown.
6. Serve hot as a side dish.

Nutrition Information (per serving): Calories: 120 Fat: 7g Saturated Fat: 1g Cholesterol: 0mg Sodium: 150mg Carbohydrates: 16g Fiber: 4g Sugar: 5g Protein: 2g

SPICY ROASTED CARROTS WITH HARISSA AND YOGURT SAUCE

Preparation Time: 10 minutes
Cook Time: 20 minutes
Servings: 4

Ingredients:

- 1 lb. carrots, peeled and sliced on the diagonal
- 2 tbsp. extra-virgin olive oil
- 1 tsp. ground cumin
- 1 tsp. paprika
- 1 tsp. harissa paste
- Salt and pepper, to taste
- 1/4 cup plain Greek yogurt
- 2 tbsp. lemon juice
- 1 clove garlic, minced

Instructions:

1. Preheat the oven to 400°F. Line a baking sheet with parchment paper.
2. Combine the carrots, olive oil, cumin, paprika, harissa, salt, and pepper in a large mixing bowl. Toss to coat the carrots evenly.

3. Spread the carrots out in a single layer on the prepared baking sheet. Place in the oven and bake for around 20-25 minutes or until the vegetables have become tender and slightly charred.
4. Whisk together the yogurt, lemon juice, and garlic in a small mixing bowl. Season with salt and pepper to taste.
5. Serve the roasted carrots with a dollop of the yogurt sauce on the side.

Nutrition Information (per serving): Calories: 140 Fat: 11g Saturated Fat: 2g Cholesterol: 5mg Sodium: 140mg Carbohydrates: 11g Fiber: 3g Sugar: 6g Protein: 4g

ROASTED CARROTS WITH TURMERIC AND GINGER

Preparation Time: 10 minutes
Cook Time: 20-25 minutes
Servings: 4

Ingredients:

- 1 lb carrots, peeled and sliced
- 2 tbsp olive oil
- 1 tsp ground turmeric
- 1 tsp grated ginger
- Salt and pepper, to taste

Instructions:

1. Preheat your oven to 400°F.
2. Combine the sliced carrots, olive oil, turmeric, ginger, salt, and pepper in a large mixing bowl. Toss until the carrots are evenly coated with the spices.
3. Transfer the coated carrots to a baking sheet lined with parchment paper and spread them out in a single layer.
4. Roast the carrots in the oven for 20-25 minutes or until tender and slightly browned.

5. Serve the roasted carrots as a side dish or garnish with fresh parsley or cilantro.

Nutrition Information per serving: Calories: 140 Fat: 11g Saturated Fat: 1.5g Cholesterol: 0mg Sodium: 250mg Carbohydrates: 12g Fiber: 4g Sugar: 5g Protein: 1g

ROASTED CARROT AND FENNEL SALAD

Preparation Time: 10 minutes
Cook Time: 20 minutes
Servings: 4

Ingredients:

- 4 medium carrots, peeled and sliced into rounds
- 1 large fennel bulb, sliced
- 2 tablespoons olive oil
- 1 teaspoon dried thyme
- 1 teaspoon dried rosemary
- Salt and pepper to taste
- 2 tablespoons balsamic vinegar
- 2 tablespoons chopped fresh parsley

Instructions:

1. Preheat oven to 400°F. Line a baking sheet with parchment paper.
2. Toss the sliced carrots and fennel in a large bowl with olive oil, thyme, rosemary, salt, and pepper.
3. Spread the vegetables out in a single layer on the prepared baking sheet.

4. Roast in the oven for 20 minutes or until the vegetables are tender and slightly browned.
5. In a small bowl, whisk together the balsamic vinegar and parsley.
6. Combine the roasted carrots and fennel with the balsamic mixture in a large serving bowl. Serve warm.

Nutrition Information (per serving): Calories: 140 Fat: 11g Saturated Fat: 1.5g Cholesterol: 0mg Sodium: 140mg Carbohydrates: 12g Fiber: 4g Sugar: 6g Protein: 2g

GRILLED ZUCCHINI WITH LEMON AND PARMESAN

Preparation Time: 10 minutes
Cook Time: 10 minutes
Servings: 4

Ingredients:

- 4 medium zucchini, sliced lengthwise
- 2 tablespoons olive oil
- Salt and pepper to taste
- 2 lemons, juiced
- 2 tablespoons freshly grated parmesan cheese
- 2 tablespoons chopped fresh basil

Instructions:

1. Preheat the grill to high heat.
2. Toss the zucchini slices with olive oil, salt, and pepper in a large bowl.
3. Place the zucchini slices on the grill and cook for 5 minutes on each side until tender and slightly charred.
4. Whisk the lemon juice, parmesan cheese, and basil in a small bowl.
5. Place the grilled zucchini on a serving platter and drizzle with the lemon-parmesan mixture. Serve immediately.

Nutrition Information (per serving): Calories: 140 Fat: 12g Saturated Fat: 2.5g Cholesterol: 5mg Sodium: 210mg Carbohydrates: 7g Fiber: 2g Sugar: 4g Protein: 4g

ROASTED CARROTS AND PARSNIPS WITH ROSEMARY AND GARLIC

Preparation Time: 10 minutes
Cook Time: 25 minutes
Servings: 4

Ingredients:

- 1 lb. carrots, peeled and sliced
- 1 lb. parsnips, peeled and sliced
- 2 tbsp. olive oil
- 2 cloves of garlic, minced
- 2 tsp. chopped fresh rosemary
- Salt and pepper to taste

Instructions:

1. Preheat the oven to 400°F. Line a baking sheet with parchment paper.
2. Combine the sliced carrots and parsnips with olive oil, minced garlic, chopped rosemary, salt, and pepper in a large mixing bowl. Toss until evenly coated.
3. Spread the vegetables out in a single layer on the prepared baking sheet.

4. Bake for 25 minutes or until the vegetables are tender and golden brown.
5. Serve immediately and enjoy!

Nutrition Information: Calories: 140 Fat: 7g Saturated Fat: 1g Cholesterol: 0mg Sodium: 240mg Carbohydrates: 20g Fiber: 5g Sugar: 10g Protein: 2g

GRILLED VEGETABLES WITH LEMON AND HERBS

Preparation Time: 10 minutes
Cook Time: 15 minutes
Servings: 4

Ingredients:

- 2 medium zucchinis, sliced
- 2 bell peppers, sliced
- 1 red onion, sliced
- 2 tablespoons olive oil
- 2 tablespoons lemon juice
- 1 teaspoon dried basil
- 1 teaspoon dried thyme
- Salt and pepper to taste

Instructions:

1. Preheat the grill to high heat.
2. Mix the sliced zucchini, bell peppers, and red onion in a large bowl.

3. Add the olive oil, lemon juice, dried basil, and dried thyme to the bowl, and mix until everything is well coated.
4. Season with salt and pepper to taste.
5. Place the mixed vegetables on the grill, and cook for about 15 minutes, occasionally flipping, until they are charred and tender.
6. Serve hot, and enjoy your delicious, anti-inflammatory side dish!

Nutrition Information (per serving): Calories: 140 Fat: 11g Saturated Fat: 1.5g Cholesterol: 0mg Sodium: 55mg Carbohydrates: 10g Fiber: 3g Sugar: 4g Protein: 2g

ROASTED CARROTS WITH CUMIN AND CORIANDER

Preparation Time: 10 minutes
Cook Time: 25 minutes
Servings: 4

Ingredients:
- 1 lb. carrots, peeled and sliced into 1/4 inch rounds
- 2 tbsp. olive oil
- 1 tsp. ground cumin
- 1 tsp. ground coriander
- 1 tsp. salt
- 1/2 tsp. black pepper
- 2 tbsp. Fresh cilantro, chopped

Instructions:
1. Preheat oven to 400°F.
2. Combine the carrots, olive oil, cumin, coriander, salt, and pepper in a large bowl. Toss until the carrots are well coated.

3. Spread the carrots in a single layer on a baking sheet. Bake for 25 minutes or until they are tender and slightly golden.
4. Remove from the oven and sprinkle with fresh cilantro. Serve warm.

Nutrition Information (per serving): Calories: 130 Fat: 11g Saturated Fat: 1.5g Cholesterol: 0mg Sodium: 600mg Carbohydrates: 10g Fiber: 3g Sugar: 4g Protein: 1g

ROASTED GARLIC AND LEMON GREEN BEANS

Preparation Time: 10 minutes

Cook Time: 15 minutes

Servings: 4

Ingredients:

- 1 pound fresh green beans, trimmed
- 4 cloves of garlic, minced
- 2 tablespoons extra-virgin olive oil
- 1 lemon, juiced
- Salt and pepper to taste
- 2 tablespoons chopped fresh parsley (optional)

Instructions:

1. Preheat oven to 400°F.
2. In a large bowl, combine the green beans, garlic, olive oil, lemon juice, salt, and pepper.
3. Toss until the green beans are evenly coated.
4. Transfer the mixture to a baking sheet and spread it into a single layer.
5. Roast for 15 minutes or until the green beans are tender and slightly charred.

6. Sprinkle with fresh parsley, if using.
7. Serve hot.

Nutrition Information per serving: Calories: 120 Fat: 11g Saturated Fat: 1.5g Cholesterol: 0mg Sodium: 200mg Carbohydrates: 9g Fiber: 4g Sugar: 3g Protein: 3g

ROASTED SWEET POTATO AND CARROT SALAD

Preparation time: 10 minutes
Cook time: 30 minutes
Servings: 4

Ingredients:

- 2 medium sweet potatoes, peeled and chopped into bite-sized pieces
- 2 medium carrots, peeled and chopped into bite-sized pieces
- 2 tablespoons olive oil
- 1/2 teaspoon salt
- 1/4 teaspoon black pepper
- 1/4 teaspoon paprika
- 2 tablespoons lemon juice
- 2 tablespoons chopped fresh parsley
- 2 tablespoons chopped fresh cilantro

Instructions:

1. Preheat oven to 425°F. Line a baking sheet with parchment paper.
2. Mix the sweet potatoes, carrots, olive oil, salt, pepper, and paprika in a large bowl.

3. Spread the vegetables in a single layer on the prepared baking sheet. Roast in the oven for 25-30 minutes or until tender and golden brown.
4. Whisk together the lemon juice, parsley, and cilantro in a small bowl.
5. Combine the roasted sweet potatoes and carrots in a large serving bowl with the lemon dressing. Serve immediately.

Nutrition Information per Serving: Calories: 200 Fat: 12g Saturated Fat: 2g Cholesterol: 0mg Sodium: 330mg Carbohydrates: 25g Fiber: 5g Sugar: 7g Protein: 2g

LEMON GARLIC ROASTED BROCCOLI

Preparation time: 10 minutes

Cook time: 20 minutes

Servings: 4

Ingredients:

- 1 head of broccoli, chopped into florets
- 2 tablespoons olive oil
- 2 cloves of garlic, minced
- 1 lemon, juiced
- Salt and pepper, to taste

Instructions:

1. Heat your oven to a temperature of 400°F (200°C) and cover a baking sheet with parchment paper.
2. Mix the broccoli, olive oil, garlic, lemon juice, salt, and pepper in a large bowl.
3. Spread the mixture out in an even layer on the prepared baking sheet.
4. Roast for 20 minutes or until the broccoli is tender and slightly charred.
5. Serve immediately.

Nutrition Information (per serving): Calories: 140 Fat: 14g Saturated Fat: 2g Cholesterol: 0mg Sodium: 160mg Carbohydrates: 9g Fiber: 3g Sugar: 3g Protein: 4g

INDIAN SPICED CARROT SOUP WITH GINGER

Preparation Time: 10 minutes
Cook Time: 25 minutes
Servings: 4

Ingredients:

- 1 tbsp. olive oil
- 1 onion, chopped
- 2 garlic cloves, minced
- 1-inch piece of ginger, peeled and grated
- 1 tsp. ground cumin
- 1 tsp. ground coriander
- 1 tsp. ground turmeric
- 1 tsp. ground cinnamon
- 1 tsp. ground paprika
- 1 tsp. ground cardamom
- 6 large carrots, peeled and chopped
- 4 cups vegetable broth

- Salt and pepper, to taste
- Yogurt or sour cream, for garnish (optional)
- Fresh cilantro for garnish (optional)

Instructions:
1. In a large saucepan, heat the olive oil over medium heat. Add the onion and cook until soft and translucent, about 5 minutes.
2. Add the garlic, ginger, cumin, coriander, turmeric, cinnamon, paprika, and cardamom, and cook for another minute, stirring constantly.
3. Add the chopped carrots and vegetable broth to the pan and boil.
4. Reduce heat and let the soup simmer for 20 minutes or until the carrots are soft.
5. Use an immersion blender or transfer the soup to a blender and blend until smooth.
6. Season with salt and pepper to taste.
7. Serve the soup hot, garnished with a dollop of yogurt or sour cream and a sprinkle of fresh cilantro, if desired.

Nutrition Information: Calories: 140 Fat: 7g Saturated Fat: 1g Cholesterol: 0mg Sodium: 420mg Carbohydrates: 19g Fiber: 5g Sugar: 9g Protein: 3g

CURRIED CHICKEN SALAD WITH SPICED CHICKPEAS AND RAITA

Preparation time: 30 minutes
Cook time: 20 minutes
Servings: 4

Ingredients:

- 2 boneless, skinless chicken breasts
- Salt and pepper
- 1 tablespoon olive oil
- 1 teaspoon ground cumin
- 1 teaspoon ground coriander
- 1 teaspoon ground turmeric
- 1/2 teaspoon ground cinnamon
- 1/4 teaspoon ground cloves
- 1/4 teaspoon ground cardamom
- 1/4 teaspoon cayenne pepper
- 1 large onion, chopped

- 3 cloves garlic, minced
- 2 cups chicken broth
- 1 can chickpeas, drained and rinsed
- 2 tablespoons Greek yogurt
- 2 tablespoons mayonnaise
- 2 tablespoons fresh lemon juice
- 2 tablespoons chopped fresh cilantro
- 2 tablespoons chopped fresh parsley
- 1/2 teaspoon sugar
- 1/2 teaspoon salt
- 1/2 teaspoon pepper
- 1 cup seedless red grapes, halved
- 1 cup diced apples
- 4 cups mixed greens

Instructions:
1. Preheat oven to 375°F (190°C). Season the chicken breasts with salt and pepper.
2. In a large skillet, heat the olive oil over medium-high heat. Add the chicken breasts and cook until browned on both sides, about 3 minutes per side.
3. Transfer the chicken to a baking sheet and bake in the preheated oven until cooked through, about 20 minutes.
4. Meanwhile, heat the olive oil over medium heat in a large saucepan. Add the cumin, coriander, turmeric, cinnamon, cloves, cardamom, and cayenne pepper. Cook for 1 minute, stirring constantly.
5. Add the onion and garlic to the saucepan and cook until softened, about 5 minutes.
6. Stir in the chicken broth and chickpeas. Bring to a boil. Reduce heat to low and simmer for 10 minutes.
7. Mix the Greek yogurt, mayonnaise, lemon juice, cilantro, parsley, sugar, salt, and pepper in a large bowl.
8. Dice the cooked chicken and add to the bowl. Add the grapes, apples, and mixed greens. Toss to combine. Serve chilled.

Nutrition Information (per serving): Calories: 450 Fat: 21g Saturated Fat: 4g Cholesterol: 80mg Sodium: 760mg Carbohydrates: 28g Fiber: 6g Sugar: 16g Protein: 36g

ARCTIC CHAR WITH CHINESE BROCCOLI AND SWEET POTATO PURÉE

Preparation Time: 15 minutes
Cook Time: 25 minutes
Servings: 4

Ingredients:

- 4 (6-ounce) Arctic char fillets
- Salt and pepper, to taste
- 1 tablespoon olive oil
- 1 tablespoon butter
- 1 large onion, chopped
- 3 garlic cloves, minced
- 1 tablespoon grated fresh ginger
- 1 tablespoon Madras curry powder
- 1 large sweet potato, peeled and cubed
- 1 cup chicken broth
- 1 cup heavy cream
- 1 bunch of Chinese broccoli, trimmed and chopped

119

Instructions:

1. Preheat oven to 400°F (200°C).
2. Season the Arctic char fillets with salt and pepper.
3. Heat the olive oil in a large oven-safe skillet over medium-high heat.
4. Add the fillets to the skillet and cook for 3-4 minutes on each side until golden brown.
5. Transfer the skillet to the oven and bake for 10-12 minutes or until the fish is cooked.
6. In a separate large saucepan, heat the butter over medium heat.
7. Add the onion, garlic, ginger, and curry powder and cook, occasionally stirring, for 5 minutes or until the onion is soft.
8. Add the sweet potato and chicken broth and bring to a boil.
9. Reduce heat and simmer for 10-12 minutes or until the sweet potato is soft.
10. Transfer the mixture to a blender and puree until smooth.
11. Return the mixture to the saucepan and stir in the heavy cream.
12. Season with salt and pepper to taste.
13. Heat 1 tablespoon of olive oil over medium-high heat in a separate large skillet.
14. Add the Chinese broccoli and cook, occasionally stirring, for 3-4 minutes or until tender.
15. Serve the Arctic char fillets with the sweet potato purée and sautéed Chinese broccoli.

Nutrition Information (per serving): Calories: 620 Fat: 38g Saturated Fat: 19g Cholesterol: 160mg Sodium: 400mg Carbohydrates: 29g Fiber: 4g Sugar: 8g Protein: 40g

PAN-SEARED SALMON ON BABY ARUGULA

Preparation Time: 10 minutes
Cook Time: 8 minutes
Servings: 4

Ingredients:

- 4 salmon fillets
- Salt and pepper
- 1 tablespoon olive oil
- 4 cups baby arugula
- 1 lemon, sliced into wedges

Instructions:

1. Season salmon fillets with salt and pepper on both sides.
2. Heat a large skillet over medium heat and add olive oil.
3. Once the oil is hot, add the salmon fillets to the skillet, skin side down.
4. Cook for 4-5 minutes on one side until the skin is crispy and golden.
5. Flip the salmon fillets and cook for 2-3 minutes on the other side or until the salmon is cooked.
6. Remove the salmon from the heat and let it rest for a minute.

7. In a large bowl, toss the baby arugula with a squeeze of lemon juice and salt and pepper to taste.
8. Divide the baby arugula between four plates.
9. Place a salmon fillet on the arugula and serve with lemon wedges.

Nutrition Information (per serving): Calories: 250 Fat: 14g Saturated Fat: 2g Cholesterol: 93mg Sodium: 140mg Carbohydrates: 4g Fiber: 2g Sugar: 1g Protein: 28g

RED BELL PEPPER, SPINACH, AND GOAT CHEESE SALAD WITH OREGANO DRESSING RECIPE

Preparation time: 10 minutes

Cook time: 0 minutes

Servings: 4

Ingredients:

- 8 ounces of baby spinach leaves
- 2 red bell peppers sliced into thin strips
- 4 ounces goat cheese, crumbled
- 1/4 cup extra-virgin olive oil
- 3 tablespoons red wine vinegar
- 2 teaspoons dried oregano
- Salt and pepper, to taste

Instructions:

1. Wash the baby spinach leaves and place them in a large salad bowl.
2. Add the sliced red bell peppers on top of the spinach.

3. Sprinkle the crumbled goat cheese on top of the red bell peppers.
4. Whisk the olive oil, vinegar, vinegar, and dried oregano in a small bowl. Season with salt and pepper to taste.
5. Pour the dressing over the salad and gently toss to combine.
6. Serve the salad immediately, and enjoy!

Nutrition Information (per serving): Calories: 300 Fat: 27g Saturated Fat: 8g Cholesterol: 19mg Sodium: 340mg Carbohydrates: 9g Fiber: 2g Sugar: 4g Protein: 10g

ROASTED BRUSSELS SPROUTS WITH POMEGRANATE AND WALNUTS

Preparation Time: 10 minutes
Cook Time: 25 minutes
Servings: 4

Ingredients:

- 1 lb. Brussels sprouts, trimmed and halved
- 1 tbsp. extra-virgin olive oil
- Salt and freshly ground black pepper
- 1/4 cup pomegranate seeds
- 1/4 cup chopped walnuts
- 1 tbsp. Freshly squeezed lemon juice

Instructions:

1. Preheat your oven to 400°F (200°C).
2. Toss the Brussels sprouts with olive oil, salt, and pepper in a large bowl.
3. Arrange the sprouts in a single layer on a large baking sheet.
4. Roast in the oven for 25 minutes or until golden brown and tender.
5. Combine the roasted Brussels sprouts with the pomegranate seeds, chopped walnuts, and lemon juice in a large serving bowl. Toss to combine.

6. Serve the roasted Brussels sprouts warm.

Nutrition Information (per serving): Calories: 150 Fat: 12g Saturated Fat: 1.5g Cholesterol: 0mg Sodium: 120mg Carbohydrates: 10g Fiber: 3g Sugar: 3g Protein: 4g

LEMON AND HERB ROASTED BRUSSELS SPROUTS

Preparation Time: 15 minutes
Cook Time: 30 minutes
Servings: 4

Ingredients:

- 1 lb. Brussels sprouts, trimmed and halved
- 2 tbsp. extra-virgin olive oil
- 1 lemon, zested and juiced
- 2 cloves of garlic, minced
- 1 tsp. dried thyme
- Salt and pepper, to taste

Instructions:

1. Heat your oven to a temperature of 400°F (200°C) and cover a baking sheet with parchment paper.
2. In a large bowl, combine the Brussels sprouts, olive oil, lemon zest, garlic, thyme, salt, and pepper. Toss until the sprouts are well coated.
3. Transfer the sprouts to the prepared baking sheet and spread them in a single layer.

4. Roast in the oven for 25 to 30 minutes or until the sprouts are tender and golden brown.
5. Remove from the oven and squeeze the lemon juice over the top. Serve immediately.

Nutrition Information (per serving): Calories: 140 Fat: 11g Saturated Fat: 1.5g Cholesterol: 0mg Sodium: 140mg Carbohydrates: 11g Fiber: 4g Sugar: 3g Protein: 4g

GRILLED EGGPLANT WITH LEMON AND HERBS

Preparation time: 10 minutes
Cook time: 10 minutes
Servings: 4

Ingredients:

- 2 medium eggplants, sliced into rounds
- 3 tablespoons olive oil
- Salt and pepper to taste
- 1 lemon, juiced
- 2 tablespoons fresh parsley, chopped
- 2 tablespoons fresh basil, chopped
- 2 tablespoons fresh oregano, chopped

Instructions:

1. Preheat your grill to medium-high heat.
2. In a large bowl, toss the eggplant rounds with olive oil, salt, and pepper.

3. Place the eggplant on the grill and cook on each side for 5-6 minutes until tender and lightly charred.
4. Mix the lemon juice, parsley, basil, and oregano in a small bowl.
5. Transfer the grilled eggplant to a serving platter and drizzle the lemon herb mixture over the top.
6. Serve hot or at room temperature.

Nutrition Information per serving: Calories: 140 Fat: 13g Saturated Fat: 2g Cholesterol: 0mg Sodium: 90mg Carbohydrates: 9g Fiber: 5g Sugar: 4g Protein: 2g

SPICY ROASTED SWEET POTATOES

Preparation Time: 10 minutes
Cook Time: 20 minutes
Servings: 4

Ingredients:

- 2 medium sweet potatoes, peeled and chopped into 1-inch pieces
- 2 tablespoons olive oil
- 1 teaspoon chili powder
- 1 teaspoon cumin
- 1/2 teaspoon paprika
- Salt, to taste
- Freshly ground black pepper, to taste
- Fresh cilantro, chopped, for garnish

Instructions:

1. Preheat the oven to 400°F.
2. Mix the sweet potatoes, olive oil, chili powder, cumin, paprika, salt, and pepper in a large bowl.
3. Spread the mixture on a baking sheet and bake for 20 minutes, flipping once, until the sweet potatoes are tender and browned.
4. Serve hot and garnished with fresh cilantro.

Nutrition Information (per serving): Calories: 190 Fat: 13g Saturated Fat: 2g Cholesterol: 0mg Sodium: 300mg Carbohydrates: 19g Fiber: 3g Sugar: 6g Protein: 2g

ROASTED SWEET POTATO AND BRUSSELS SPROUTS SALAD

Preparation Time: 15 minutes
Cooking Time: 30 minutes
Servings: 4

Ingredients:

- 2 large sweet potatoes, peeled and diced
- 1 pound brussels sprouts, trimmed and halved
- 1 red onion, chopped
- 2 tablespoons olive oil
- Salt and pepper, to taste
- 1/4 cup balsamic vinegar
- 2 tablespoons Dijon mustard
- 2 tablespoons honey
- 4 ounces of baby spinach
- 1/4 cup pecans, toasted and chopped

Instructions:

1. Preheat the oven to 400°F.
2. Mix the sweet potatoes, brussels sprouts, red onion, olive oil, salt, and pepper in a large bowl.
3. Transfer the mixture to a large baking sheet and bake for 25-30 minutes or until the vegetables are tender and slightly caramelized.
4. Whisk the balsamic vinegar, Dijon mustard, and honey in a small bowl.
5. Mix the roasted vegetables, baby spinach, pecans, and balsamic vinaigrette in a large bowl.
6. Serve immediately.

Nutrition Information per serving:

Calories: 280, Fat: 18g, Saturated Fat: 2g, Cholesterol: 0mg, Sodium: 120mg, Carbohydrates: 30g, Fiber: 5g, Sugar: 15g, Protein: 5g

ROASTED CAULIFLOWER AND QUINOA SALAD

Preparation time: 10 minutes

Cook time: 30 minutes

Servings: 4

Ingredients:

- 1 head of cauliflower, chopped into florets
- 1 cup of quinoa
- 2 tablespoons of olive oil
- 1 teaspoon of garlic powder
- Salt and pepper to taste
- 1/4 cup of chopped parsley
- 1/4 cup of crumbled feta cheese
- 1/4 cup of sliced almonds
- 2 tablespoons of lemon juice
- 1 tablespoon of honey

Instructions:

1. Preheat the oven to 400°F.
2. Toss the cauliflower florets in a large mixing bowl with 1 tablespoon of olive oil, garlic powder, salt, and pepper.
3. Spread the cauliflower in a single layer on a baking sheet and roast for 25-30 minutes or until tender and golden.
4. While the cauliflower is roasting, cook the quinoa according to the instructions.
5. Combine the roasted cauliflower, cooked quinoa, chopped parsley, crumbled feta cheese, and sliced almonds in a large serving bowl.
6. Whisk the lemon juice, honey, and 1 tablespoon of olive oil in a small mixing bowl.
7. Drizzle the dressing over the cauliflower and quinoa mixture and toss to combine.

Nutrition Information per serving: Calories: 380 Fat: 18g Saturated Fat: 3g Cholesterol: 10mg Sodium: 160mg Carbohydrates: 49g Fiber: 7g Sugar: 8g Protein: 12g

DESSERTS

SPICED POACHED PEARS WITH ALMOND CREAM

Preparation Time: 15 minutes
Cook Time: 20 minutes
Servings: 4

Ingredients:

- 4 medium pears, peeled and cored
- 1 cup water
- 1 cup unsweetened almond milk
- 1/2 cup maple syrup
- 1 cinnamon stick
- 2 whole cloves
- 1/2 teaspoon ground ginger
- 1/4 teaspoon ground nutmeg
- 1/4 teaspoon ground allspice
- 1/2 cup almonds, chopped
- 1/2 cup plain Greek yogurt

Instructions:

1. Combine the water, almond milk, maple syrup, cinnamon stick, cloves, ginger, nutmeg, and allspice in a medium saucepan. Stir to combine.
2. Add the pears to the saucepan and simmer over medium heat. Cover and simmer for 15-20 minutes or until the pears are soft and tender.
3. In a food processor, process the almonds until they are finely chopped.
4. Mix the chopped almonds and Greek yogurt in a small bowl. Stir to combine.
5. Serve the poached pears in bowls with a dollop of almond cream.

Nutrition Information per serving: Calories: 220 Fat: 8g Saturated Fat: 1g Cholesterol: 0mg Sodium: 20mg Carbohydrates: 39g Fiber: 7g Sugar: 28g Protein: 7g

BAKED CINNAMON APPLES WITH WALNUTS

Preparation Time: 10 minutes
Cook Time: 25 minutes
Servings: 4

Ingredients:

- 4 medium apples, cored and sliced
- 1/4 cup walnuts, chopped
- 2 tbsp. pure maple syrup
- 2 tsp. cinnamon
- 1/4 tsp. nutmeg
- 1 tsp. vanilla extract
- Pinch of salt

Instructions:

1. Before starting to cook, heat your oven to 375°F (190°C)
2. Mix the sliced apples, walnuts, maple syrup, cinnamon, nutmeg, vanilla extract, and salt in a large bowl.
3. Transfer the mixture to a 9x9 inch (23x23 cm) baking dish.

4. Bake for 25 minutes or until the apples are tender and the mixture is fragrant.
5. If desired, serve the baked apples warm with a scoop of vanilla ice cream.

Nutrition Information per serving: Calories: 185 Fat: 9g Saturated Fat: 1g Cholesterol: 0mg Sodium: 15mg Carbohydrates: 28g Fiber: 4g Sugar: 21g Protein: 2g

CHOCOLATE AVOCADO PUDDING

Preparation time: 10 minutes

Cook time: 0 minutes

Servings: 4

Ingredients:
- 2 ripe avocados
- 1/2 cup unsweetened cocoa powder
- 1/2 cup maple syrup
- 1 teaspoon vanilla extract
- 1/4 teaspoon salt
- 1/2 cup almond milk

Instructions:
1. Pit the avocados and scoop the flesh into a blender or food processor.
2. Add the cocoa powder, maple syrup, vanilla extract, salt, and almond milk. Blend until smooth and creamy.
3. Taste and adjust the sweetness and seasoning as needed.
4. Divide the pudding into serving bowls and chill in the refrigerator for at least 30 minutes before serving.

Nutrition Information per serving: Calories: 260 Fat: 18g Saturated Fat: 2g Cholesterol: 0mg
Sodium: 115mg Carbohydrates: 29g Fiber: 9g Sugar: 17g Protein: 4g

CINNAMON SPICED APPLE AND ALMOND CRUMBLE

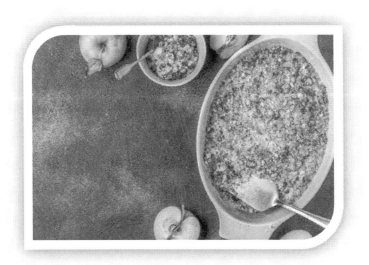

Preparation Time: 10 minutes

Cook Time: 30 minutes

Servings: 6

Ingredients:

- 4 medium apples, peeled and chopped into small pieces
- 1 tsp ground cinnamon
- 2 tbsp pure maple syrup
- 1 cup almond flour
- 1/2 cup rolled oats
- 1/4 cup chopped almonds
- 1/4 cup coconut sugar
- 1/4 tsp salt
- 1/4 tsp baking powder
- 6 tbsp unsalted butter, melted

Instructions:

1. Preheat your oven to 375°F (190°C).

2. Mix the chopped apples, cinnamon, and maple syrup in a large bowl.
3. Mix the almond flour, oats, chopped almonds, coconut sugar, salt, and baking powder in a separate bowl.
4. Pour the melted butter into the dry ingredients and mix until well combined.
5. Transfer the apple mixture to a 9x9 inch (23x23 cm) baking dish.
6. Sprinkle the crumble mixture evenly over the apples.
7. Bake for 30 minutes or until the top is golden brown and the apples are tender.
8. Serve warm with a scoop of ice cream or a dollop of whipped cream, if desired.

Nutrition Information: Calories: 364 Fat: 26g Saturated Fat: 12g Cholesterol: 48mg Sodium: 121mg Carbohydrates: 31g Fiber: 5g Sugar: 20g Protein: 6g

BLUEBERRY & ALMOND CHIA PUDDING

Preparation Time: 10 minutes

Cook Time: 2 hours (for chilling in the fridge)

Servings: 4

Ingredients:

- 2 cups almond milk
- 1/2 cup chia seeds
- 1/4 cup honey
- 1 tsp vanilla extract
- 1 cup fresh blueberries
- 1/4 cup slivered almonds
- Fresh mint leaves (optional)

Instructions:

1. Whisk the almond milk, chia seeds, honey, and vanilla extract in a medium bowl until well combined.
2. Stir in the blueberries.

3. After covering the bowl, refrigerate it for at least 2 hours, or leave it overnight until the chia seeds have soaked up the liquid and the mixture has become thick.
4. Serve the chia pudding in bowls, topped with slivered almonds and a sprinkle of fresh mint leaves, if desired.

Nutrition Information (per serving): Calories: 210 Fat: 12g Saturated Fat: 1g Cholesterol: 0mg Sodium: 70mg Carbohydrates: 22g Fiber: 7g Sugar: 13g Protein: 6g

SPICED BERRY COMPOTE WITH ALMOND CRUMBLE

Preparation time: 10 minutes
Cook time: 20 minutes
Servings: 4

Ingredients:

- 1 cup mixed berries (strawberries, blueberries, raspberries)
- 1 tbsp maple syrup
- 1 tsp cinnamon
- 1/4 tsp nutmeg
- 1/4 tsp allspice
- 1 tsp cornstarch
- 1 tbsp water
- 1/2 cup almonds
- 1/4 cup rolled oats
- 1 tbsp coconut oil
- 1 tbsp maple syrup
- 1/4 tsp salt

Instructions:

1. Combine the mixed berries, 1 tbsp maple syrup, cinnamon, nutmeg, and allspice in a medium saucepan. Cook over medium heat for 5-7 minutes, until the berries break down and release their juices.
2. Mix the cornstarch and water in a small bowl to make a slurry. Pour the slurry into the saucepan with the berries and stir well.
3. Cook for another 2-3 minutes until the mixture thickens. Remove from heat and set aside.
4. In a food processor, pulse the almonds, oats, coconut oil, 1 tbsp maple syrup, and salt until the mixture resembles coarse crumbs.
5. To serve, divide the berry compote among 4 serving dishes and sprinkle the almond crumble over the top. Enjoy!

Nutrition Information (per serving): Calories: 252 Fat: 16g Saturated Fat: 4g Cholesterol: 0mg Sodium: 123mg Carbohydrates: 25g Fiber: 6g Sugar: 12g Protein: 6g

ROASTED GRAPE AND ALMOND TART

Preparation Time: 20 minutes

Cook Time: 25 minutes

Servings: 8

Ingredients:

- 1 cup whole wheat flour
- 1/4 cup almond flour
- 1/4 cup coconut sugar
- 1/4 teaspoon salt
- 1/2 cup cold unsalted butter, cubed
- 1 egg yolk
- 1 teaspoon vanilla extract
- 2 cups red grapes, halved
- 2 tablespoons honey
- 1 tablespoon olive oil
- 1/4 teaspoon cinnamon
- 1/4 teaspoon nutmeg
- 1/4 teaspoon allspice
- 1/4 cup sliced almonds

- 1 tablespoon lemon juice

Instructions:

1. Preheat oven to 400°F. Line a 9-inch tart pan with parchment paper.
2. Mix the whole wheat flour, almond flour, coconut sugar, and salt in a large bowl.
3. Cut in the cold butter until the mixture resembles coarse crumbs.
4. Mix in the egg yolk and vanilla extract until a dough forms.
5. Press the dough evenly into the bottom and sides of the tart pan. Bake for 15 minutes.
6. Meanwhile, mix the grapes, honey, olive oil, cinnamon, nutmeg, and allspice in a separate bowl.
7. Spread the grape mixture over the crust, sprinkle with sliced almonds, and drizzle with lemon juice.
8. Bake for 10 minutes or until the grapes are roasted, and the crust is golden brown.
9. Serve warm or at room temperature.

Nutrition Information (per serving): Calories: 300 Fat: 19g Saturated Fat: 9g Cholesterol: 55mg Sodium: 180mg Carbohydrates: 32g Fiber: 2g Sugar: 17g Protein: 5g

ROASTED PEACH AND RASPBERRY SORBET

Preparation time: 10 minutes

Cook time: 15 minutes

Servings: 4

Ingredients:

- 4 ripe peaches
- 1 cup raspberries
- 1/4 cup honey
- 2 tablespoons fresh lemon juice
- 1 teaspoon lemon zest
- 1/4 teaspoon ground cinnamon

Instructions:
1. Preheat the oven to 375°F.
2. Cut the peaches in half and remove the pit. Place the peaches cut-side up on a baking sheet lined with parchment paper.
3. Mix the raspberries, honey, lemon juice, lemon zest, and cinnamon in a small bowl. Spoon the mixture over the peaches.
4. Roast the peaches for 15 minutes or until they are soft and tender.
5. Remove the peaches from the oven and let them cool for 10 minutes.

6. Puree the peaches and raspberry mixture until smooth in a blender or food processor.
7. Pour the mixture into a container and freeze for 2 hours, stirring every 30 minutes.
8. Scoop the sorbet into serving dishes and enjoy!

Nutrition Information (per serving): Calories: 170 Fat: 1g Saturated Fat: 0g Cholesterol: 0mg Sodium: 0mg Carbohydrates: 43g Fiber: 3g Sugar: 36g Protein: 2g

BAKED CINNAMON APPLES RECIPE

Preparation Time: 15 minutes

Cook Time: 25 minutes

Servings: 4

Ingredients:

- 4 medium apples, peeled, cored, and sliced
- 2 tablespoons coconut sugar
- 2 teaspoons cinnamon
- 1 tablespoon grass-fed butter or coconut oil
- 2 tablespoons water
- 1 teaspoon vanilla extract
- Optional toppings: chopped nuts, coconut cream, or dairy-free ice cream

Instructions:

1. Preheat oven to 375°F (190°C).
2. Combine the sliced apples, coconut sugar, cinnamon, butter or coconut oil, water, and vanilla extract in a mixing bowl.
3. Transfer the mixture to a 9x9-inch baking dish.

154

4. Bake in the oven for 25 minutes or until the apples are tender and the top is golden brown.
5. Serve warm with your preferred toppings, if desired.

Nutrition Information: Calories: 165 Fat: 7g Saturated Fat: 4g Cholesterol: 15mg Sodium: 5mg Carbohydrates: 29g Fiber: 4g Sugar: 23g Protein: 1g

ROASTED STRAWBERRY AND RHUBARB COMPOTE WITH CHIA SEEDS AND ALMOND MILK

Preparation Time: 10 minutes
Cook Time: 20 minutes
Servings: 4

Ingredients:

- 1 lb strawberries, hulled and halved
- 1 lb rhubarb, sliced
- 1/4 cup maple syrup
- 1 tsp vanilla extract
- 1 tsp grated fresh ginger
- 1/4 tsp salt
- 1/4 cup chia seeds
- 2 cups unsweetened almond milk

Instructions:

1. Preheat oven to 375°F (190°C).

2. Mix the strawberries, rhubarb, maple syrup, vanilla extract, ginger, and salt in a large baking dish.
3. Roast in the oven for 20 minutes or until the fruit is soft and the syrup is bubbly.
4. In a medium bowl, mix the chia seeds and almond milk. Let sit for 5-10 minutes until the mixture thickens into a pudding-like consistency.
5. Serve the roasted fruit warm, topped with a spoonful of chia seed pudding.

Nutrition Information (per serving): Calories: 250 Fat: 10g Saturated Fat: 1g Cholesterol: 0mg Sodium: 145mg Carbohydrates: 40g Fiber: 8g Sugar: 28g Protein: 7g

CINNAMON ROASTED APPLE WITH ALMOND BUTTER

Preparation time: 10 minutes

Cook time: 25 minutes

Servings: 4

Ingredients:

- 4 medium-sized apples, peeled, cored, and sliced
- 1 tbsp. cinnamon
- 1 tbsp. honey
- 1 tbsp. coconut oil
- 1 tsp. vanilla extract
- 1/4 tsp. salt
- 1/4 cup almond butter

Instructions:

1. Preheat oven to 375°F (190°C).
2. Mix the sliced apples, cinnamon, honey, coconut oil, vanilla extract, and salt in a large bowl.

3. Transfer the mixture to a baking dish and bake for 25 minutes, occasionally stirring, until the apples are tender and slightly caramelized.
4. Serve the roasted apples warm, topped with almond butter.

Nutrition Information (per serving): Calories: 270 Fat: 20g Saturated Fat: 5g Cholesterol: 0mg Sodium: 110mg Carbohydrates: 25g Fiber: 5g Sugar: 19g Protein: 5g

BEVERAGES

GREEN TEA, GINGER, AND LIME INFUSION

Preparation time: 5 minutes
Cook time: 5 minutes
Servings: 1

Ingredients:
- 1 cup of water
- 1 green tea bag
- 1-inch piece of fresh ginger, sliced
- 1/2 a lime, juiced

Instructions:
1. Boil the water in a small saucepan.
2. Once the water reaches boiling point, remove the saucepan from the heat and add the green tea bag and ginger slices.
3. Let the tea steep for 3-5 minutes.
4. Remove the tea bag and ginger slices, and add the lime juice.
5. Stir to combine and let the tea cool to room temperature.
6. Serve the tea over ice and enjoy.

Nutrition information (per serving): Calories: 10 Fat: 0g Saturated Fat: 0g Cholesterol: 0mg Sodium: 0mg Carbohydrates: 3g Fiber: 0g Sugar: 2g Protein: 0g

SPICED TURMERIC MILK

Preparation time: 5 minutes

Cook time: 5 minutes

Servings: 1

Ingredients:

- 1 cup almond milk
- 1 tsp honey
- 1 tsp ground turmeric
- 1/4 tsp ground cinnamon
- 1/4 tsp ground ginger
- Pinch of black pepper
- Optional: 1 tsp vanilla extract

Instructions:

1. Heat the almond milk over medium heat in a small saucepan until a simmer.
2. Add the honey, turmeric, cinnamon, ginger, and black pepper to the milk. Stir to combine.
3. If desired, add the vanilla extract.
4. Cook for a few minutes, occasionally stirring until the mixture is heated.
5. Pour the mixture into a mug and enjoy!

This drink is delicious and a great way to get the anti-inflammatory benefits of turmeric, ginger, and cinnamon. The black pepper helps to enhance the absorption of the turmeric, and the honey adds a touch of sweetness. Enjoy this drink as a warm and comforting way to end your meal.

SPICED TURMERIC LATTE

Preparation Time: 5 minutes
Cook Time: 5 minutes
Servings: 1

Ingredients:

- 1 cup unsweetened almond milk
- 1 teaspoon turmeric powder
- 1/2 teaspoon ground cinnamon
- 1/4 teaspoon ground ginger
- 1/4 teaspoon ground cardamom
- 1/4 teaspoon ground black pepper
- 1 teaspoon honey (optional)
- 1 shot of espresso or 1/4 cup of strong coffee (optional)

Instructions:

1. In a small saucepan, heat the almond milk over medium heat until steaming.
2. Add the turmeric, cinnamon, ginger, cardamom, and black pepper to the saucepan and whisk until well combined.
3. Reduce the heat to low and let the mixture simmer for 2-3 minutes, stirring occasionally.
4. Add honey, espresso, or coffee to the saucepan and stir until well combined.

5. Pour the mixture into a mug and enjoy.

Nutrition Information (per serving): Calories: 70 Fat: 4g Carbohydrates: 8g Protein: 2g Sugar: 6g Fiber: 1g Sodium: 170mg

TURMERIC GINGER TEA

Preparation Time: 5 minutes
Cook Time: 10 minutes
Servings: 1 serving

Ingredients:

- 1 cup water
- 1-inch fresh ginger root, peeled and sliced
- 1-inch fresh turmeric root, peeled and sliced
- 1 tbsp honey
- 1 tsp lemon juice

Instructions:

1. Bring the water, ginger, and turmeric to a boil in a small saucepan.
2. Reduce heat and let the mixture simmer for 10 minutes.
3. Strain the mixture into a cup and add the honey and lemon juice. Stir until the honey is fully dissolved.
4. Enjoy the warm tea.

Nutrition Info (per serving): Calories: 64 Fat: 0.1 g Carbohydrates: 16.5 g Protein: 0.5 g Fiber: 0.8 g Sugar: 13.5 g

ANTI-INFLAMMATORY GINGER, TURMERIC AND LEMON DRINK

Preparation Time: 5 minutes
Cook Time: 5 minutes
Servings: 1 serving

Ingredients:

- 1-inch fresh ginger, peeled and grated
- 1-inch fresh turmeric, peeled and grated
- 1 lemon, juiced
- 1 tsp honey (optional)
- 1 cup water

Instructions:

1. Combine the grated ginger, turmeric, lemon juice, honey, and water in a small saucepan.
2. Bring the mixture to a boil, then reduce the heat and let it simmer for 5 minutes.
3. Strain the mixture into a mug and enjoy hot.

This drink is a great way to help reduce inflammation in the body, thanks to the anti-inflammatory properties of ginger and turmeric. The lemon adds a burst of vitamin C, which can also help to reduce inflammation. The honey is optional, but it does add a touch of sweetness to balance out the spicy flavors of ginger and turmeric.

GREEN ANTI-INFLAMMATORY SMOOTHIE

Preparation time: 10 minutes

Cook time: None

Servings: 1

Ingredients:

- 1 banana
- 1 cup spinach
- 1/2 avocado
- 1/2 inch ginger
- 1/2 lemon, juiced
- 1 cup unsweetened almond milk
- 1/2 teaspoon honey (optional)
- 1/2 teaspoon turmeric
- 1/2 teaspoon cinnamon

Instructions:

1. Combine all the ingredients in a blender and blend until a smooth mixture is formed

2. Pour the mixture into a glass and enjoy immediately.

Nutrition Info (per serving): Calories: 297 Fat: 19g Carbohydrates: 33g Protein: 5g Fiber: 10g Sugar: 15g

This green smoothie is packed with anti-inflammatory ingredients like turmeric, ginger, and cinnamon, as well as healthy fats from the avocado and fiber from the spinach and banana. Lemon juice boosts vitamin C, which helps support a healthy immune system. Almond milk makes the smoothie creamy and provides a good source of calcium and other nutrients!

SPICED APPLE CIDER

Preparation time: 5 minutes

Cook time: 5 minutes

Servings: 2

Ingredients:

- 4 cups of fresh apple juice
- 2 cinnamon sticks
- 1 tsp. of freshly grated ginger
- 4 cloves
- 1 tsp. of honey
- 1 tsp. Of freshly squeezed lemon juice

Instructions:

1. Add apple juice, cinnamon sticks, ginger, and cloves in a medium saucepan.
2. Heat the mixture over medium heat until it boils.
3. Minimize the heat and let it simmer for 5 minutes.
4. Take the saucepan off the heat source and allow it to cool down for approximately 2-3 minutes.
5. Stir in the honey and lemon juice.

6. Using a fine mesh strainer, strain the mixture into two glasses.
7. Serve the spiced apple cider warm, and enjoy!

Nutrition Information (per serving): Calories: 135 Fat: 0.5g Carbohydrates: 33g Protein: 1g Fiber: 3g

GREEN APPLE GINGER ANTI-INFLAMMATORY SMOOTHIE

Preparation time: 10 minutes

Cook time: None

Servings: 2

Ingredients:

- 1 medium green apple, cored and chopped
- 1 banana
- 1-inch piece of ginger, peeled and chopped
- 1 cup of spinach
- 1/2 cup unsweetened almond milk
- 1/2 cup water
- 1 tbsp. honey
- 1 tsp. chia seeds

Instructions:

1. Add the green apple, banana, ginger, spinach, almond milk, water, honey, and chia seeds into a blender.
2. Blend the ingredients on high speed until smooth and well combined.
3. Divide the smoothie into two glasses and serve immediately.

Nutrition information (per serving):

- Calories: 175, Total Fat: 4g, Saturated Fat: 0g, Cholesterol: 0mg, Sodium: 50mg, Total Carbohydrates: 36g, Dietary Fiber: 4g, Sugar: 24g, Protein: 3g

TURMERIC GINGER ELIXIR

Preparation time: 5 minutes

Cook time: 0 minutes

Servings: 1

Ingredients:

- 1 cup of water
- One piece of fresh ginger, about one inch in size, peeled and grated.
- 1-inch piece of fresh turmeric, peeled and grated
- 1 lemon, juiced
- 1 tsp honey (optional)
- Pinch of black pepper

Instructions:

1. Boil the water in a small saucepan.
2. Add the grated ginger and turmeric to the boiling water.
3. Lower the heat and allow the mixture to simmer for 3-5 minutes.
4. Strain the mixture into a cup and add lemon juice to taste.

5. Add honey (if desired) and a pinch of black pepper.
6. Stir well and enjoy your anti-inflammatory turmeric ginger elixir.

This drink is rich in antioxidants and anti-inflammatory compounds and has a warm and spicy flavor. The combination of turmeric and ginger is particularly effective in reducing inflammation. Additionally, lemon juice and black pepper help to enhance the absorption of turmeric.

CONCLUSION

The Anti-Inflammatory Diet Cookbook provides a comprehensive guide to incorporating anti-inflammatory ingredients into your daily diet. It offers a variety of recipes for breakfast, snacks, entrees, sides, desserts, and drinks, all designed to promote overall health and wellness by reducing inflammation in the body. The recipes feature ingredients known for their anti-inflammatory properties, such as turmeric, ginger, omega-3-rich fatty acids, and antioxidants. Additionally, the cookbook provides helpful information on the preparation time, nutrition information, cook time, and serving size for each recipe. This cookbook offers a variety of delectable and nourishing meal choices that can assist you in reaching your health objectives, whether you're looking to enhance your overall well-being, manage a long-standing condition, or adopt a more balanced and healthier diet.

Made in the USA
Las Vegas, NV
26 April 2023

71087301R00101